CW01511328

It All Makes Sense Now

Charting a young woman's spiritual journey inspired by an angelic visitation.

Jane Litchmore-Grant

PRESS

It All Makes Sense Now
Charting a young woman's spiritual journey inspired by an angelic visitation.
by Jane Litchmore-Grant

Printed in the United States of America.

ISBN 9781498481939

www.xulonpress.com

Acknowledgement

*T*hanks be to the Almighty God for His inspiration and guidance. Special recognition for the angelic visitation which inspired this book.

To my darling husband, Linton Grant, who has been my encourager even when the chips were low and I felt like giving up. Also for providing the photographs included.

To my lovely children Janel, Abbigail and Joshua who tried to keep out of my hair so I could concentrate on my writing. Thanks for the maturity you showed.

To my dear friend Veronica Trotman-Roberts who provided support with the children and encouragement along the way.

To my dear friend Pastor Marlene Williams who often checked on my progress although living so far away from me.

To my dear friends John and Helen Richardson, secretary to Churches Together in Hitchin for believing in me and giving me constant encouragement.

To Bishop Dr Joe Aldred, with responsibility for Pentecostal and Multicultural Relations at Churches Together in England, for your encouragement and advice; and whose work as an author inspires me on this journey.

Special thanks to my dear friends Chelsea and Judith who proof read and edited my work. Your efforts and commitment are greatly appreciated.

Dedication

*T*his book is dedicated to my dear family who have had to put up with me during this whole process – Rev Linton Grant, Janel, Abbigail and Joshua.

I dedicate all the praise, glory and honour to the Holy Spirit who have protected and guided my life in my walk of faith in Him, which enables me to say 'It All Makes Sense Now'.

Contents

Preface

The Inspiration

This book has been inspired by a very beautiful 'next-to-perfect looking' young lady who unexpectedly visited me at my home in 2006 (Marsh Farm, Bedfordshire). The shocking scenario surrounding this visitor is still largely unexplainable. I have since personally taken two slants on this visit, which I will explain in a moment – strange and remarkable.

It started out being a beautiful day. But by mid-morning a freak storm was forecasted on the weather bulletin. Approximately 2 hours later, amidst the hustling sounds of the strong winds, I heard the door bell ringing. When I went to see who it was I was greeted by a beautiful young woman seeking shelter from the storm, as the bus stop across from my house, where she was sheltering was unsafe. She was actually awaiting a bus at the time the storm arrived.

We did have a good conversation about the storm, which caused her to seek shelter at my home in the first place; and about life. I was rather curious as to how well she knew me and my husband, Linton, based on the many things she shared with me that day. However, the most remarkable thing about my 'visitor' was that before she left, she told me that I needed to write the experiences I have been journaling into a book. That immediately got my attention. But her subsequent statements to really grabbed me. They were more like instructions. She said to me:

"You must write about your experiences!"

To which I responded. "You know, that is interesting; because I have indeed been journaling for some time now."

Then she said to me:

"You have been journaling for some time now, from about the year 2000. You need to write your experiences into a book and **the title of your book should be: IT ALL MAKES SENSE NOW.**"

"Wow!" I thought. It is true; I had been journaling since 2000. But how did she know that? How did she know so much about me and my husband? Who is she?

So when she mentioned the title I should give my book. That arouse my suspicion.

Her statements rendered me numb for a few minutes. It was a shock to me. I thought to myself: 'This stranger just gave me a title for my pending book!'

It is ironic that only a couple months before the Holy Spirit impressed upon me to write a book. The fact is that being an author has been a long-time dream of mine. So since the prompting of the Holy Spirit, I have been praying about the format this book will take and very importantly, what the title should be. Therefore, this statement from a 'perfect stranger' did instantly stand out for me. Was this a coincidence? I don't think so. It really startled me; but I realised now that it was not a coincidence. Rather, I believe this was what I would call a 'God incidence'–a God appointed moment for me.

For quite a few months, I have been seriously considering 'a title' that I could give to my writings. There was such a sense of urgency. I knew I needed to write a book 'now'; and had even mentioned my ambition to my husband. I had also gone as far as to speak to an artist about designing a cover for me. But, believe it or not, I never even had a title. Can you imagine? Possibly, this was a perfect case of 'Putting the cart before the horse' here.

The Big Question! This unusual visit raises a big question in my mind. How did she know that I was even writing–well journaling, since the year 2000?

The truth is, I knew that I very much wanted to write a book – it was my big dream. I however, was really struggling to find firstly, the time to sit down and do it. Given that I had a one year old baby and two other young children. Secondly, I was struggling to find a title for my writings and experiences, in effect my autobiography. Up to this point I had been reciting titles and even cover designs over and over in my mind; but just could not come up with anything suitable. Now here is the answer being presented to me by a complete stranger– just like that! Isn't that Amazing?

Prologue

My Remarkable and Strange Visitor. Was this an Angel?

———— ⟨☉⟩ ————

*I*n my opinion this visit was two-fold–It was **remarkable** and it was **strange**! 'Remarkable', because I can remember all the details of her visit, as though it was yesterday. The only exception is that I cannot remember this lady's name; only that it begins with a 'C'. Christine? No! Carol? No! Catherine? No! I just can't remember what she said her name was. Remarkable!

It was 'strange' how she knew so many specific details about both my husband and I. Information about our experiences not just here in the UK but also about our lives back home in Jamaica as well. She said she knew my husband, Linton 'very well' (She even named him). So I asked her where she knew him from. She told me that they might have crossed paths at his former workplaces–Garmex HEART Academy in Jamaica,

National Training Agency NTA or Seaforth High School, she couldn't say for sure but she knows him 'very well'. She advised that I should ask him about her when he gets home, and she told me her name. (Only I can't remember it, once she left). She knew where we lived in Jamaica, where we both worked, where we pastored, how we came here with according to her 'two cute babies and their helper'. All the time I am thinking, how does she really know so much about us, about Linton yes... but me?—Especially since I have never laid eyes on her before.

Another 'strange' feature of this visit and visitor was that I did not see where the 'fine lady visitor' disappeared to after she left our home. As soon as she left through the back door of our house, I hurriedly went upstairs to look through the living room window (a proper vantage point) to watch her walk to the bus stop across the road from our house. But to my surprise, she was nowhere to be seen. She was not at the bus stop. She was not walking down the street. She was not walking up the road either. No bus had passed yet, neither was there anyone at the bus stop. I could see her nowhere. Nobody was there. Strange! Very strange! Remarkable!

This visit, coupled with my life-long ambition of becoming a writer, has finally caught up with me. So despite my many roles and increasing responsibilities as a wife, mother, part-time teacher and now a co-pastor

I was determined to come out of my comfort zone and get cracking; all-be-it these many years later.

As a wife, mother of three young children, part-time teacher, parent governor at my daughters' school, Women Ministry Director, Sunday School Superintendent and teacher, church PRO director and assistant to my husband, Linton, who has been serving as a pastor in the United Kingdom, my plate was prover-bially full. So this book is birth out of a life of dedication, commitment and hard work. Bearing in mind that this beautiful 'Lady C...' visited me when our son Joshua was only about 11 months old, the title which she gave me—'It All Makes Sense Now'- does make some sense to me, now.

Often when one goes through challenging 'issues' one can't seem to appreciate or make sense of them, without keeping one's eyes on the outcome. This is like looking for the 'light at the end of the tunnel'. I just could not make sense of much of my experiences while going through them. Hardly anyone can, anyway. Some of these were daunting experiences related to migration, as one can image. The one thing I was assured of was my determination to follow the instruction to see where it leads.

By implication this title, IT ALL MAKES SENSE NOW, allows for retrospection. Being able to look back in order to make sense of what had gone on before. This has allowed me to come in agreement with God's plan for my life. Certainly in retrospect, these many years later, all those experiences do 'make sense now' and are still 'making sense' today. Well even better sense, today.

My Motivation

*M*y motivation for this book is for the purpose of giving praise, honour and glory to God the Father and to my Lord and Saviour Jesus Christ. Each of the stories shared in this book is aimed to ultimately give praise and glory to God. Psalm 50:23 states "Whoso offereth praise glorifieth me: and to him that ordereth his conversation aright will I shew the salvation of God." (KJV)

It is my hope to praise God on a wide scale. I join with David in Psalm 35 v 18 (KJV) in saying: "I will give thee thanks in the great congregation. I will praise thee among much people."

Often in the British culture it has been somewhat tricky for me to share my testimony face to face. The opportunity was not always readily available.

It is also my hope that other people (Christians and non-Christians) who have had similar trying experiences or are even encountering them presently, will be encouraged and empowered. James encourages: 'Knowing this, that the trying of your faith worketh patience. But let patience have her perfect work, that ye may be perfect and entire." (James 3:3-4 KJV) It all makes sense now!

Chapter One

Family Background

*B*orn in Above Rocks, St Catherine, Jamaica, West Indies, I am privileged to be writing this book from over 6,000 miles away from home. I was born out of an adulterous relationship but I believe that my brother, Tony (also a product of the same relationship) and I were purposed to be here in our family for a time like this. Our mum and dad made 'mistakes'- choir member and deacon had a 'thing going on' which had its consequences.

I am sure they were not proud of their behaviour but here we are. It may not have made sense to them then, but it sure does make sense now. So my brother and I, the end products of this relationship, became the hidden children of the Litchmore family. This resulted in occasional visits from our father (who was a married man), then eventually, a non-existent father. So when he died it seemed no difference to us at all because unfortunately, we were used to not seeing him around anyway.

I am the third of six children for my mum and the first girl. I am thankful to God for my five fantastic siblings who all played a role in building my character. My grandparents were instrumental in my up-bringing because they took me from my mother at a very early age in order for her to focus on the other children. In those days I lived at the 'top house' and visited 'bottom house' (Mama's house); often having two dinners. That was the fun part. However, my life was to change quite suddenly when at the death of my grandmother I was back living with Mama at the age of 10 and half.

During childhood, we were poor – not having much money, but our home had lots of love. My grandfather was that father I did not have. God rest his soul. He was very gifted and worked hard to take care of his family thus helping us to maintain a good status in our community. My grandmother, God rest her soul, must still hear her name being called by us daily. She led us as a family in the ways of the Lord and was a true prayer warrior. She taught my cousin and I (the girls in the family) to be industrious, well-mannered and tidy. The boys would get off a bit lighter, but were taught to be responsible and accountable by her.

I still recall some of the strong measures taken by her to ensure we got things right. For example, I remember the time when the clothes she asked us to wash were not done to the approval of our Granny. We were to find out when she called us to the clothes line only to find the wet clothes on the ground. She then explained that she had opened the clothes pegs and let them fall to the ground so we know which ones weren't washed properly. We were fuming. Angry, ashamed and disappointed, we were forced to pick up the wet clothes from the ground and rewash them. You could not possibly believe how relieved we were when our washing got her approval. Rough treatment, bless her, but it seemed to have worked. Also I strongly believe her intentions were pure.

Granny taught me to pray from an early age and she conducted weekly family prayer meetings. Mama, her only daughter, tried to carry on where she left off after her death following a motor vehicle accident. I noticed something with my mother which was questionable. Often when my Mama had pains in her body she would place my hand on the place where it hurt while she would pray. I really wanted to ask her about why she did it but in those days children did not ask adults why they did what they did. It was the era of the belief where 'children are seen and not heard'. However, me being a very inquisitive child – often being told that I ask too many questions – finally asked my mother why she did that. She explained to me that one day she felt the leading of the Holy Spirit to place my hand on the source of her pain while she prayed. She said that to her surprise her pain was instantly gone. So since then whenever she felt pain she would place my hand on her body while she would pray.

Even this act of faith was something I was being taught, unconsciously by my mother. At the time it made absolutely no sense to me. But now it is makes spiritual sense, as I see the Lord works miracles by the laying on of my hand on some occasions.

My faith walk began from an early age. The family attended church with our grandparents who were Baptist Union members. Grandfather was a member of the church choir and Granny was an ardent member who was known for hospitality in the church and in the community. She often used me to be the carrier of gifts to the shut-ins in the community. To be honest, often I didn't feel like doing it; especially because I had to walk long distances to these homes. Please remember that I was not walking on paved roads either.

Fitting Into my Granny's Gift-giving Missions to Shut-Ins

I had to walk through bushy paths after heavy dew falls coupled with burr-burr sticking to the tail of my dress. (For those who had no idea what burr-burr are.

They are sticky blossoms which attach themselves to fabric upon contact. It's a real chore to remove them – more like a menace.) Often I would pray a version of prayer somewhat like Jesus did in his agony 'Father let this cup pass from me'. I confess, sometimes Granny would call me to go on these 'giving missions' I would pretend to be sleeping and had to be literally yanked out of bed.

Again, it made no sense to me then. Except that I sometimes felt I was being punished. But the happiness I felt when these shut-ins would smile when they saw me arrive with their cooked breakfasts and groceries over powered the negative emotions. It was a pleasure just to watch them eat as their teeth less jaws went up and down making the food appear even more delicious than ever. These acts began to make sense to me, far outweighing what I originally felt as punishment. As these people normally would have no living relative nearby, we became their extended family. They often thanked me with words like "God bless you and Aunt Doris, Annie. May your food- basket never be empty." As a youngster these words sound good to the ears but had no more meaning to me then; so I would return home and tell my Granny what these people had said. I am sure she made sense of their sayings. They do make sense to me now.

I Did Not Get Away With Lying

If I thought I would get away with anything, when dealing with my Grandmother, I had to think again. Believe me, I tried it and I failed miserably. One day while at home I felt I wanted a piece of the freshly baked hard dough bread. It had been cut before so I thought no one would even notice I had taken some. Why I did not think to ask my grandmother I have no clue. However, I thought I would be clever about it.

No sooner than I finished cutting the bread I could hear my granny's footsteps approaching the kitchen. Flip, flap, flip, and flap. I quickly threw the bread into the nearby mortar and covered it with a kitchen towel in an effort to hide it from granny. To my dismay, she was coming directly to use the same mortar. She wanted to continue pounding the cocoa beans she had left unfinished the night before. My grandmother used to make chocolate for sale at the weekly market. These were made from cocoa beans after being parched and pounded, then made into balls rolled between the palms. Unique trade!

But I had a problem on my hand. Why did granny have to come to the mortar in which I had disguised the bread? And why did she have to come at that precise time? So as she approached the mortar I knew I had to lie to get out of this situation. So, without hesitation I lied that I was not the one who put the bread in the mortar when I was asked how the bread got there. Well, it goes without saying that it was me, because as granny said 'Well you and I are the only ones here, and it's not me; so it must be you.' How could I have thought to lie to my grandmother? Why would I have thought to take the bread without asking in the first place? She would have given it to me once I asked anyway, so there was absolutely no need to steal.

The lesson I learned from this experience lives with me for ever. After a good lecture on how 'liar and thief walk together', Granny walked away. Soon she returned with a ruler and with its edge she hit me on my knuckles while she recited the gem 'Speak the truth and speak it ever. . . ' The punishment lasted while she slowly she recited it. The idea was so that it took longer while at the same time I was getting more hits. Who says grannies aren't clever? Yes, it was very painful, but it was meant to be, in order to teach me a valuable lesson. Thankfully that lesson stayed with me.

The spiritual guidance I received from my grand-parents and my mum has left an indelible mark on me. Possibly its influence was why I accepted the Lord at a tender age. (Read more about this in My Call and Miracle of Salvation – testimonies). Leaving the Baptist church was a decision I made with my older brothers and cousin who preferred the fellowship at the 'little

Church of God Sunday School class' which was started in our community at the time. We felt it was more lively and the people were more friendly; a conviction I still hold even today, although I believe things are improving.

Chapter Two

Career Background

$\mathcal{A}$s a child my mother saw me as a nurse and often encouraged me to pursue that career path because of what she saw as a 'helpful demeanour' in me. However, it never was something I aspired to as I did not like the sight of blood. Although I had some bad examples of the teaching profession, I found myself often teaching objects around the house. I guess I was determined to be the opposite of those 'mean teachers'. While growing up at home I cannot count the times my siblings caught me off guard, of course, speaking in my 'teaching voice' to various objects around the house. I recall the time my big brother, Macky, surprised me with his loud burst of laughter after he observed me dressed in Mama's shoes, ear rings, bangles, handbag and a stick with my book in hand teaching drinks bottles. These bottles were arranged in a line and when

I impersonated the answers incorrectly I would strap them. When the bottles would hit on each other, I (teacher) would shout at them "Stop the crying!" My brother did try his best to contain himself but he could no longer hold his laughter. And he has a healthy laugh. Subsequently, he taunted me with this joke for a very long time. But thankfully it never deterred me from my ambition of becoming a teacher.

In school I happened to perform well and was awarded a scholarship to High school at age 11. During High School I maintained high academic performances and attained first place awards from first form to third form. Unfortunately, due to different constraints, I did not do as well as I expected during my GCE and CXC examinations. There was much I had to deal with at school–some of which I explain later. Emotionally, I suffered from anxiety. I remember having headaches and fainting spells during my first external examination. After being given a pain killer by an examination official, I must have fallen off to sleep because when I woke up I was just in time to hear the invigilator announcing: 'You have 15 minutes to finish'. So I literally wrote that paper in fifteen minutes. Needless to say it was a miracle I came out with a Grade 111 in CXC English Language (which was like GCSE grade C).

After I left high school I was attracted to the Mico Teacher Training College and wished I could go there.

As I did not have the exam grades to qualify for entry I applied to the National Training Agency on the job training programme. As I had indicated on my resume that my first choice of career was to become a teacher, I happen to be given a placement to work in the General Office of the Mico Teachers College. Coincidence? I don't think so. So after working as a clerk/typist to the principal's secretary for 2 years and 7 months I enrolled as a preliminary student. While working I redid some exams to gain better grades but was not successful. There was too much going on in my life at the time, especially in relation to living arrangements becoming unbearable. I had moved from a rural area of the island to stay with a friend of my Mum. Unfortunately, it did not work out well in the end. But I was not to be deterred. So, I decided to quit working and go into teacher training full time.

In 1991 I graduated in fine style from the one of the world's oldest teacher training institutions – the Mico College. Surprising to me, I was awarded 4 times at my graduation. The printry responsible for printing our graduation programmes was burnt down the Thursday prior to our graduation – just three days prior to the actual graduation ceremony. So can you imagine the shock I got when at our graduation I was taken out of the general queue to the awards section? None of the graudants had programmes neither did any of us have a clue as to what was going to happen on the day. A friend of mine borrowed a tutor's programme so we could check what our awards were for. It was unbelievable to see my name coming up 4 times. My testimony on Mico Fees Miracle will help you to understand why 'my name' here was shocking for me. Yes, IT ALL MAKES SENSE NOW!

The awards I received on my graduation day did not only stun me but also my dear mama. She was literally in tears as she watched me collect them one after the other. She must have been thinking that her 'partner money' used to send me to college was not in vain. Bless her, she went against her own desires for me becoming a nurse and supported me in pursuing my dream of becoming a teacher. The awards included: Dedication to Special Education, Outstanding Research in Deaf Education, Most Improved and Disciplined Student (Female) and a cash award. Is this a miracle or what?

As I reflect on these awards, I am reminded of the young man who was awarded the male counterpart of the Most Improved and Disciplined Student (Male). We happened to be good friends while in college. So when we realised we were both awarded for these awards, he joked to me that evening: "It seems like the Miss Terry's produced 'disciplined children' around here. You see, both our mums happened to be called 'Miss Terry'. Interesting co-incidence! Or maybe not.

Upon graduating from teachers' college I was head hunted by the school where I did my practicum twice. Firstly, I was appointed provisionally then after six months I was permanently employed. Over the next seven years I received a few promotions from provisional to senior teacher level two. I served in this position for seven years. My final promotion came at the point at which I was in the process of migrating to the UK, after being at the school for eleven years.

Unfortunately, I did not even get to take up the post, because as it turned out, I was on a plane to England a couple weeks prior to the date my new post would have become effective. Sounds crazy I know. And maybe it was at the time; but when I look back, God had a plan. (See more about this in my testimony during CTH chairman's inauguration speech).

There has been a real struggle for me in the area of my career since migrating to the UK. Much of what we were told by the agency about working in the UK turned out to be far from reality. I have had many setbacks and disappointment in so much as I have decided to change my career after being in education for twenty-five years. It is a very daunting prospect and often confusing. It is hard to let go of what you know for the unknown especially after some wonderful experiences as a teacher from the very start.

My first job as a teacher was rewarding, not so much in terms of money, but in terms of the number of lives I was to have touched over the eleven years I worked at the school. Then, later the two and a half years full time and ten years part-time experiences here in the UK, have undoubtedly extended that greatly–despite being many and varied. Needless to say, some have left me thinking what next?

These experiences have helped me to come to a decision. After all, when I see the many doors being slammed in my face and yet I kept pushing (studying, taking courses, volunteering et cetera). Now my spiritual intuition has kicked in and I am beginning to believe it is time for a change. I even heard a whisper of the Holy Spirit: 'I shut doors that no man can open and I open doors that no man can close.' I have started to take notice.

During the time at home with my baby I started a masters course in psychology with the Open University. It was very challenging and costly too. At the time of my enrolment I was not yet a citizen, so I had to enrol as an overseas student. That meant I had to pay far more fees than the British students. Tutorials were held at he university campus in Cambridge. I would leave my baby and family and travel by train or coach to tutorials in Cambridge at least once per month. It took me four years to complete the masters degree, but I am so thankful to the Lord I persevered and did it. It is my hope to be able to use it to find work in the area of psychology in the very near future.

For me the sense of fulfilment on reaching this milestone was immense. Often I wonder 'how can I make sense of this?' But if you have been home as a stay at home mum you will find any achievement fulfilling. It is making sense now!

Sign Language Ministry

As an extension to my career as a teacher of the deaf (TOD), a Sign Language Ministry was birthed in Jamaica. Inspired from my work on television and working with the performing groups from school, I felt the need to purposely target deaf and hearing impaired people for the kingdom of God. On seeing the need to minster to the deaf and hearing impaired in our nation, I felt a compulsion to host free sign language classes to young people from my church with the passion. This later extended to other church groups – empowering them with the communication tools to witness to the deaf of our nation.

You just never know how far a simple idea can go. Well I certainly had no idea. From these classes I was to be invited to teach Sign Language to other groups (religious and non-religious) including former Miss Jamaica/ World, Kathy Levy's youth group and the Portmore Vision Choir (over 100 voices). God has truly blessed this idea and many churches in Jamaica today use Sign Language as an art form to minister to young people – deaf and hearing alike.

Coming to the UK this gift was figuratively, put on a shelf. This art form was not popular here. However, after seven years of not using the gift God has revived me and I have had to push down cultural barriers and have offered performances on a few occasions since then. By God's grace there is more to be done. God is not through with me yet.

Chapter Three

Charting My Spiritual Journey

―――● ⟨⊙⊙⟩ ●―――

*MY CALL TO BAPTISM IN THE HOLY GHOST

MY CALL

As a child I became conscious of my soul and God at an early age–6 years old. In the 1970s many evangelists and pastors did preach about the reality of heaven and hell. And who wants to go to hell? So initially my desire to serve the Lord was more to avoid hell rather than a true understanding of His love for me. I started requesting water baptism since then.

MY SALVATION MIRACLE

A remarkable thing happened when I was 7 years old. No, I did not get my water baptism, but my pet dog died and I felt responsible for it. My pet Chihuahua had just eaten 3 of Grandma's 6 tiny day-old chicks. Overcome with grief and loss my cousin and I, aged 6 and 7 at the time, respectively, decided to discipline her for her actions. Our actions, however, led to her accidental death and my big brother, Macky, taunted me day and night. Repeatedly resounding in my ears I would hear his voice saying:

" Hell shall be your portion; hell shall be your portion!...

You killed little Chi-wee-wee. Hell shall be your portion."

('Chi-wee-wee' was my pet name for the puppy – my way of pronouncing 'Chihuahua').

At my next visit to church, I was the first person at the altar praying for forgiveness and loudly confessing what I had done. I felt a peace and a comfort that I was not able to explain as I felt the tears rolling down my face. ***This was my miracle***. I knew the Holy Spirit did touch me that day. As I was crying and praying out loudly, I sometimes heard outbursts of laughter and chuckles from the congregation. Afterwards I came to realise that the people were indeed laughing at me. It did not matter to me then, I was intent on getting out of hell, (as I felt that's where I was) into heaven – a place of peace, even if it meant being scuffed at.

I still marvel at the way I came to find peace at such early age. Today 34 years later I testify, the peace of

God truly surpasses our human understanding, as stated by Paul. "And the peace of God, which passeth all understanding, shall keep your hearts and minds through Christ Jesus." (Phil 4:7 KJV) Therefore, being in this place of peace I requested water baptism. But at the time my granddad thought I was far too young to be baptised. I was so disappointed. 'Too young' was never something I even thought about. However, he promised I would be baptised the following year and I believed him.

However, next year came and went. Again my grandfather said 'You are too young, next year you can do it.' That never happened. In fact it took 3 years to the fulfilment of this promise. So you can just imagine the excitement I had when my grandmother announced to me that it was fine for me to take my water baptism that morning.

MY WATER BAPTISM AT LAST!

At age 10 I finally had my water baptism. My grand-dad kept putting off my request year after year until finally my grandma decided to help me. She came up with a very clever plan. She hid my white dress in her hand bag and brought it down to the river where the baptism was to be taking place. Delighted that I was going to finally experience my heart's desire, having been put off for 3 years, I eagerly walked to the church where a service was held before we proceeded to the baptismal session at the river.

Back in those days, baptisms were conducted by the river; not in a pool like we do today. I can still recall my grandmother's words when it was over:

"Well let your Grandpa take the water off you now."

That began my journey with the Lord as that same evening I was given 'the Right Hand of Fellowship.' This meant that I officially became a member of the Church of God of Prophecy, on March 20th 1977.

One of the remarkable things I remembered from this baptismal service was a woman I call Miss Myrtle standing in the crowd, saying I was too 'little' to be taking water baptism. She felt I would, according to her, 'be back out in the world (backslidden) in just two weeks' time'. Hard as that sounded then, I knew better than to believe her. In fact it has challenged me and I endeavoured to prove this lady wrong. Since then all during my Christian journey, as soon as I was tempted, the first face and voice I saw and heard was that of Miss Myrtle. To God be the glory! I am still in the race today, 34 years later.

Yes, I was a little and petite, 10 year old girl who did not know much then, but I was certain that God loved me and that Jesus was coming back. In those days it was common to hear preachers preaching about hell fire and brimstone. So, yes, it is true my dread of hell was heightened then. But thankfully, my decision to follow Christ was much earlier than hearing these messages. But at the same time, I did not want to go to hell, the place of 'torments' according to Luke 16:23.

TESTING DAYS WERE TO FOLLOW BAPTISM

The following day after my water baptism I was to be surprised by a group of friends whom I thought would have been happy for me. Unfortunately, their reaction was far from what I was expecting. A member of my class called me and said that she heard that I was baptised yesterday to which I happily answered in the affirmative. She then suddenly grabbed my hand and started to twist my hand saying I have to curse a 'bad word' (expletives) or she wouldn't stop twisting my hand. It was painful but I turned to her and said "It doesn't matter what you do to me I will not curse." So she and the others started to jeer me and laughed at me saying "Where is your God now?" as they pulled my plaits, twisted my arms and just having fun.

Somehow in the agony I felt the presence of God in a real way. Everything stopped hurting and I calmly said to them "Even if you kill me I will not curse a bad word or curse God." Such words coming from my 10 year old self was astonishing. Where did such boldness come from? Now I knew it was from God the Father. The girls got weary of me not responding to their pulling and tugging and finally gave up. Yes, you heard me right, they left me alone. Since that day none of them ever troubled me again. Instead, they went around the school saying that I was a true Christian. The same girl even went as far as to inform my teacher of my water baptism. Thankfully, my teacher was delighted for me!

It was a gruelling start to my journey with the Lord but that experience, although it never made sense to me at the time, does *make perfect sense to me now!* Thank you Lord!

The SUPERNATURAL continues

At the age of 12 and 13 I recall two eventful moments which led me to the conclusion, "It's Supernatural!" Firstly, I was given my first appointment in church as a Sunday school teacher of the junior class. My pastor must have seen something in me which I never saw; so for me that was 'supernatural.' During this time, I did learn to lean on the arms of the Lord, Jesus. Thanks be to God, He has enabled me to teach scores of children and numerous lives were touched and changed. Small wonder therefore, I went on to becoming a teacher and doing so for 20 years and going.

Baptism in the Holy Spirit – Quite an experience

Secondly, was my baptism with the Holy Spirit. I was one of a group of girls who found it humorous when people were 'speaking in unknown language' or what the Bible refers to as 'speaking in tongues'. We would sometimes even do imitations of specific people's tongues. "Eat up the cho-cho-cho!" for example. However, during one of the highly spiritually charged services, what used to be called 'tarrying service,' I had a life changing experience. Suddenly, the tongues and activities which used to amuse me, did not feel humorous any more. I could not bring myself to laugh at the people speaking in tongues as there was an uneasiness about my doing so.

During this time I suddenly saw what appeared to be a bright light which appeared in front of me as a peaceful presence overshadowed me. This is the brightest light I have ever seen. In the end, I too was speaking in another language,.

This is an experience that is hard to explain. But what I can say is that it felt strange. I suddenly felt like a heavy load was lifted off my shoulders. My friends later explained to me what they witnessed happened with me. They explained that it was as though a bright light had shone on my face and I was transformed before their eyes. It was then that they became conscious that

I was not faking or joking around but that this was real and serious. As a result, they started praying ('reaching out' as it was called then) and they vowed never to laugh at people who speak in tongues or those who are slain in the spirit ever again. Thank you Lord! You used my life to change others for the better.

Part One

Chapter Four

Testimony Time – From Jamaica

*MY NEAR DEATH EXPERIENCE – IT'S SUPERNATURAL!

*W*hen I testify, it is to give praise to God for the things He has done in my life. I am reminded of Revelation 12:11 which says: "And they conquered him by the blood of the Lamb and the word of their testimony, and they did not love their lives until death." Also the word of the Lord states in Psalm 19:7b – "The testimony of the Lord is sure, making wise the simple." (NKJV)

As I grow older, I find it more helpful not to leave things solely to memory as we often forget. So I decided to put them in writing, as Alison Krauss says in the chorus of her song, Remind Me Dear Lord:

'Roll back the curtains of memory now and then.

Show me where you brought me from and where I could have been.

Just remember I'm human and humans forget.

So remind me, remind me, Dear Lord.'

After scanning the lyrics of the above song they also remind me of a song I had heard as a child: 'Memories don't leave like people do; they always stay with you, whether the thing be good or bad' (by Johnny Bristol). Therefore I think it best to scribe while these memories are with me. "I decree and I declare over all who will come in contact with this book that you and I will always have the ability to remember. I decree also that we are blessed with the spirit of a 'sound mind' in Jesus' mighty name! Amen."

Much has happened in my life which brings glory to God. Some of these events I am not proud of or never did make sense of, but in the end God gets the glory. I will attempt to relate some of these great experiences and challenges in stages, as far as I can remember because 'it all makes sense now!'

MY NEAR DEATH EXPERIENCE – IT'S SUPERNATURAL

When I was 9 years old my family believed I was brought back to life. This event was witnessed by my mother and grandmother, other members of the family and neighbours. They agreed with me that **this was indeed supernatural**! I did not understand exactly what it was then, until (as an adult) I learnt about 'out of body experiences.' As I was declared dead by those around my bedside, I believe this experience is correctly described as 'my near death experience'.

As I lay sick in bed at home suffering from dengue haemorrhagic fever (DHF) or 'break-bone fever' as it was commonly called, I had an extraordinary experience. I witnessed my body (it felt like a lighter version of my physical body) hovering over my real body on the bed. In shock I pondered how could I have two bodies? (Or so it seemed at the time). I looked down on the body on the bed and the top of the heads of everyone gathered in the room. I just felt myself being lifted up and up to the ceiling, somewhat like riding an escalator, only I was still in a lying position.

In the ceiling, I could see no one but I could hear audible voices as if two people were arguing. There was a disagreement as to whether I should 'stay' or 'go back'. It felt like two opposing forces were fighting for ownership of me. Among what seemed to me to be confusion, I heard a clear and steady voice saying: "No! No! No! I am not through with her yet!" At this point I saw my floating 'lighter body' re-entering my physical body as it laid in the bed, where my family had gathered in prayer. I then heard my grandmother shouting: "Thank you Lord! Thank you Lord for bringing Annie back to us!"

Everybody were crying, screaming and shouting praises to God. Now I could see their faces and not the tops of their heads. I was later told that I had been non responsive and my body bore the signs of being dead for several minutes. Grandma and Mama thought God had brought me back from the dead. Subsequent to explaining to Grandma what had happened she explained that this 'lighter body' (I referred to previously) was indeed my spirit which had temporarily left my body.

That sounded very creepy. I had never heard of anything like that before. When I became an adult I heard more than one accounts of 'near-death-experiences' or 'out of body experiences' with which I can identify. I was reminded of my own experience as I now realise that I was not alone.

Dengue haemorrhagic fever (DHF) had left many sufferers dead in Jamaica during the mid to late 70s. Our community was badly affected. Through this miraculous work of God I was spared; so to God be the glory. Today my testimony is: "Thank God for a praying mother and grandmother."

Chapter Five

Supernatural Deliverance From Poison

*THE HEALING MIRACLE – MORE THAN A MIRACLE
*THE POISON PLOT FINALLY REVEALED
*THE POWER OF FORGIVENESS

Shortly after my 13th birthday and after my Holy Spirit infilling, the Lord miraculously delivered me from a poisonous plot to take my life. In high school I started to see God's favour on my life. I happened to have scored high grades in successive classes. This led to me being awarded first placement in my class for three successive years. So I went from 3rd stream to 1st stream, an achievement most people would normally celebrate with you. But what I did not know was that one class mate (Patsy, not her real name) found it offensive and devised a plan to take me out of the scene, literally to kill me. Only I did not know it at that time.

It is still perplexing to conceive how such a young girl could have thought of such an evil plan and executed it so well. We were in third form in high school, comparable to year 9 in the UK. Go with me down memory lane.

Our end of term test results had just been published and our subject teachers had come to give us our feed backs. As it was my first time passing history at that level, the teacher called me to her desk and commended me on my efforts. On my way back to my seat a classmate made an unpleasant comment. Her exact words **in** the Jamaican patois were:

"Every test dat de gal deh tek she pass it. Her Mumma mus a wuk obeah".

That is to say in English, 'every test that that girl takes she passes it. Her mother must be involved in witchcraft.'

My initial thoughts were to ignore her and not to allow such negative statement to penetrate my mind. But at the end of the lesson my girlfriend, Janet warned me to be weary of the girl with these evil thoughts, because of the terrible thoughts she expressed in the lesson that day. From now on I will refer to her as 'Patsy'.

Several weeks later it was clear to me that Patsy wanted nothing to do with me and she was not prepared to be quiet about it. As girls in our early teens, there were somethings that were easily recognisable to us.

There were some irritating behaviours which alerted me to a dramatic change in Patsy's behaviour. Her actions involved shifting her clothing when I happen to passed by her, 'cutting of eyes', turning of the head and using insulting remarks. I ignored them all.

One day during the mango season another friend of mine, whom I will call 'Girly' (not her real name), came and offered me a large ripe East Indian mango. She told me she had been to the country to visit relatives for the weekend and brought me back the mango. The story sounded true, so I took the mango and thanked her for thinking of me.

After taking the mango from her, I started walking down the stairs towards my classroom. Shortly afterwards my entire body started shaking. Then the trembling got more violent. My feet and arms were trembling uncontrollably. I was frightened. My friend Janet with whom I was walking at the time noticed my trembling body and made an alarm.

"What's wrong with you Jane?" She enquired.

Trembling I replied:

"I don't know, since I received this mango from Girly my body just started trembling".

Then I thought not to eat it and to throw it away. But my friend would not have any of it. She then asked me to give it to her rather than throwing it away because it smelled so good. I strongly refused.

"If it is making me feel like this it might do the same to you," I said to my friend, Janet.

So I quickly decided to toss the mango away. Remarkably, as soon as the mango left my trembling hand my body instantly calmed down. It was unbelievable.

Neither Janet nor I said anything about this incident. But remarkably, I started noticing a change in Patsy's behaviour when she saw me over the ensuing days. Over the next day I noticed a visibly shocked Patsy when she saw me. She appeared even more shocked displaying clear expressions of fright and disbelief on the few days following the incident. It was then that I thought back to the mango scenario.

"Could she be linked in any way to that mango Girly had given me?" I thought.

You guessed it. I was spot on – right indeed! Janet and I called Girly and quizzed her about that mango she had given me earlier that week. Immediately she tried to dodge my question but when she realised how serious I was, she broke down crying. In tears she revealed to us that she had lied to me. She explained that Patsy had indeed given her the mango to give to me. But she had also warned her not to let me know it was coming from her, as she wanted to surprise me. Then I asked about her **own** story of 'going to the country,' to which she replied:

"That too was a lie; we made it up so you could believe me. Is something wrong?"

"Wrong? Of course something is very wrong!" I screamed back at her.

"That could have harmed me, you know. I did not eat it because of my body's reaction. But when I saw the shock on Patsy's face upon seeing me on the ensuing days following, it suddenly dawned on me that something was definitely wrong. That is why I thought Patsy might have had something to do with this 'gift' of a mango."

Girly's question–Is something wrong?" made me realised that she was being used as a friend of mine to administer the poison. There was no way Patsy would have attempted to offer me a gift directly, given the terrible thing she had said about me earlier and in the presence of our classmates, regarding my test results.

I did however wonder: How could Girly not have picked up on Patsy's evil plot? I then realised that she was naïve, so I could not blame her. I just thank God for having delivered me on that day. It was only through the power of God that I was speared, as there was absolutely no other way for me to have known something was wrong with that 'mango.' Thank you Lord! Feel free to join me in giving a big praise to God for His divine protection over my life. Thank you Lord! Certainly God specialises in things that seem impossible.

What I did not know was that a great testimony was to have emerged later from my encounter with this same young lady, Patsy.

THE HEALING MIRACLE – MORE THAN A MIRACLE
PATSY'S MUM GOT A HEALING MIRACLE

Probably about 6 months or so later, as my friend Janet and I were walking home from school, we were alerted by the screams of a little boy running down the road crying for someone to help his mother. We immediately rushed towards him and as we got closer we realised he was half naked – no shirt on. We asked him what the matter was. Between sobs he told us that his mother had 'dropped down' and she could not talk. So thinking she might have fainted we ran with the little boy to his home where we found his mother slumped over her bed with half of her body hanging off. She was hardly breathing.

I tried to find out what had happened her but she was only able to say a few broken words "Je-sus, Je-sus". She could not speak a complete word let alone explain anything. We were unsure of what to do at this point. Suddenly, the Holy Spirit directed me to do what I saw my grandmother and mother did when someone is sick. Pray. Janet and I laid hands on this strange lady (as we did not know her) and we prayed as sincerely as any 13 and 14 year-old girls could. That was the first thing we thought of doing and truthfully, we were afraid she was dying.

Before I continue, let me set the scene. In this community back then there were very few people who owned a motor vehicle. However, one of these owners lived rather closely to this lady's house. So that was another option we had if she needed to be rushed to the hospital (which is over 19 miles away). But A MIRACLE HAPPENED right before our eyes. And to know that God had graciously used me in this way! As soon as we were finished praying and said "Amen" the lady opened her eyes and took a deep breath. She looked a bit wild as she said to us "Where am I?" (This was said without breaking in her breath). Then she asked: "Who are you?"

We explained to her how her son had come running down the road crying for someone to help his mother and how we rushed to her house and found her hanging off your bed. We told her that she could not speak and that she was hardly breathing. Then she proceeded to explain exactly what has happened to her. She was exposed to wood smoke and being asthmatic, she had a severe attack. She said that as soon as she felt her chest tightening she ran to the bed room and only got as far as the foot of the bed when she passed out.

She was so thankful for us coming in and helping and praying for her. We quickly suggested that she gives some credit to her son who ran out on the road, half naked, to find help. Brave little lad indeed!

All this time neither my friend Janet nor I knew who this lady was, as she and her family had only recently moved to this part of the district. However, what was to be revealed later would be both shocking and enlightening. This was indeed a very powerful revelation for me. That is the reason I refer to this as 'More than a miracle'. It was in fact two miracles which happened in front of us that day.

THE POISON PLOT FINALLY REVEALED!

In her thankful and 'happy to be alive' moment Paty's mum looked at us and asked who we were? She asked which family do we 'belong to'? Janet told her about her parents and grandparents who were known to Mrs O B. (Patsy's mum. Not her real initials.) Then she asked me: "Who do you belong to?" As I began to tell her my mother's name she interrupted: "Theresa Robinson is your mother?" I answered in the affirmative. She then asked "That means Mass Ewan is your grandfather?" I told her "Yes, he is my grandfather." Her eyes bulged and with both hands on her head she blurted out "Lawd God have mercy! Mi did tell O B (not her husband's real name) nuh fi do it!" (In English that means: I had told OB not to do it). This statement made absolutely no sense to me. So looking very confused I asked her "You told your husband not to do what Miss?"

As she explained to me and my friend Janet, we were both shocked, disappointed and yet happy at the same time – a proper mixed emotions here. Mrs O B's account of the incident brought answers to a lot of questions I obviously had since that day I was given the mango. You see, *this woman happened to be Patsy's mother*. Remember, Patsy was the girl who disguised a mango and gave it to one of my friends to give to me some six months prior. Wow! What a shock! As Mrs O B continued to give her account of the incident to us, all the questions I had about 'the mystery mango' were being answered.

This was such a revelation! Until this day we could not explain what had happened to the mango and neither could we say for sure how Patsy was involved. Although we knew for sure she was directly involved, we did not know the details. Now in her own home everything is being explained from 'the horse's mouth' as it were. Patsy's mother explained how that her daughter came home speaking about me and how bright I was. Instead of being happy for me she became jealous and enraged that I was passing all my tests and she wasn't. She would go on and on about it and then one day her dad promised to bring this all to an end. This decision, according to Mrs O B, she had strongly disagreed with. But they carried on with it despite her strong opposition.

Then finally she 'spilled the bean'–the mango was poisoned! Her husband and daughter had made a plot to let my friend administer it to me. Because, at that time her daughter was no longer speaking to me in school, for her to offer me something to eat, would be suspicious. Earlier, she had even tried to fight me at school during her 'period of hatred towards me' – a David and goliath experience.

Upon hearing such confession, Janet and I looked at each other in utter bewilderment. My mouth must have fallen open, I just could not believe what I was hearing and witnessing. Then I thought 'What is a 14 year old to do with such shocking information? The truth is I was NUMB! Shocked and disappointed for a while I managed to say to her: "Good thing I had not died, or God could not have used me here today to pray healing over you."

Immediately, Mrs O B burst out crying. Janet and I rubbed her back and told her "Never mind!" In fact all three of us were crying at this point. The presence of the Lord entered that room. I found myself praying for myself – "Lord please forgive these people. Please help me to forgive them. Then I started to pray for her husband and also for Patsy who was still at school at the time (probably doing athletic training). She was the school's champion runner.

What a revelation!!! It still give me the creeps today, so many years after.

THE POWER OF FORGIVENESS
Result–Patsy's Family Receives Salvation

When one goes through trying situations it always seems endless. For me nothing was making sense to me at the time. Why would anyone want to kill me just because God has blessed me with intelligence and talents? However, after meeting with the family who tried to kill me I instantly decided to forgive them. It was not easy but I did ask God to help me, right there and then. Especially seeing how God used me to pray healing over her and saw he healed before my eyes, my decision to forgive was not as hard as per normal. Then I thought to take the opportunity to invite the family to our church's week of crusade which was being held that same week. It just so happened that they lived not too far from the church.

That week a remarkable miracle happened! I was not sure if they would come to the crusade but I saw them approaching the tent from a far. I was so happy to see them turn up. I rejoice today for the *power of forgiveness* because as a result of it a great miracle resulted. Four members of Patsy's family gave their hearts to the Lord including her mum and dad. She was to follow a few weeks later – as the crusade was extended. To God be the glory!!!

So out of a bad situation I witnessed several miracles, my life being supernaturally speared, Patsy's mum being speared from sudden death and now the mighty miracle of salvation for four members of their family. 'Praise the Lord!' I invite you to praise Him with me! As I reflect on the whole scenario I am reminded of Joseph's experience where he said in Gen 50:20:

'But as for you, you meant evil against me; *but* God meant it for good, in order to bring it about as *it is* this day, to save many people alive.' My God is awesome indeed!!! (NKJV)

Chapter Six

God Failed My Suicide Attempt

*T*his next account has been my personal secret for many years. There is nothing honourable about suicide so it took great courage and divine intervention for me to break my 29 year old secret. Not even my husband was let into this 'top secret' prior to our marriage. You see, 'suicide is not something a Christian does'. Or so I thought. So although God supernaturally delivered me from sure death at the time, I felt shame, guilt and unworthiness for many years. I just could not share it.

Thankfully the Holy Spirit revealed to me how all these 29 years of keeping this testimony a secret has robbed God of the glory He deserved. He challenged me that He already knows the whole thing from the start anyway, so why bother to hide or cover it up? The scales were instantly removed and my eyes became opened. Since then it no longer hurt to share this testimony. Even though I seldom do, no more pain is associated with it.

What happened was that a few months before my seventeenth birthday I was forced into a position which made me think there was no point to living. I bought into the enemy's lies and sadly when that happens, it never end well. After all, the thief comes only to steal, kill and to destroy. But Jesus says "I have come that you may have life and have it more abundantly." (John 10:10 KJV)

The New Living Translation puts it this way: 'The thief comes only to steal and kill and destroy; I have come that they may have life, and have it to the full.'

In retrospect, I am convinced that God had a better plan for my life. Jeremiah 29:11 (NLT) affirms: 'For I know the thoughts that I think toward you, says the LORD, thoughts of peace and not of evil, to give you a future and a hope.'

The situation was that my life was fine. I was enjoying my young life and after a couple years of a good solid friendship with my first boyfriend, we had our first major disagreement. To give you a background, this young man was firstly a fabulous friend and confidant. His mother and siblings loved and respected me very much. These sentiments were mutual from my side of the family too. We were often referred to as 'a match made in heaven.'

As he started to make demands on me that I could not, rather was not prepared to offer, based on my Christian principles, things started to change. One day out of frustration I told him to go and find someone else who can give him what he desired. The truth is I meant it; but had no idea he would actually do it. In fact I was hoping he would not. A 'girl thing', I presume. I guess what I really meant was that he would stop bothering me but not to go find another.

So my mum noticed that he no longer came to visit me and asked what was happening between us. I was forced to face my fears and so I told her that I had asked him to leave me alone (but did not tell her exactly why), so he won't be coming here again. It was not long that I got the shock of my life. He started showing off his new found love and boy, did he not flaunt it in my face. Both our mums were not very pleased but we had to live with our decisions. I started to feel the rejection so deeply that I became withdrawn. I even started to think that I might have done the wrong thing in turning the guy away out of my life and could not deal with the con-sequences. So on top of the rejection I was feeling at the time, I started blaming myself – the 'blame game'. I prayed and prayed but just could not break free from it.

But things came to a head one day when I was alone at home (good condition, I thought) and I just happened to see a piece of equipment that belonged to this friend. That brought memories of him back to my mind – a dangerous thing. Suddenly I thought to myself, I do not want to continue living and I can use his own dagger to end my life – to end the pain of rejection and the sense of loss. I planned exactly what I was going to do and how I was going to do it. I rehearsed it so it would not fail.

As I got ready to commit the act in the back room of our house, I felt the need to get a pen and paper to write a letter to my Mum – to explain why I had to do what I was about to do. It was only fair that when she returned from the market and found my body she would know why and would not be too angry with me. So as I raised myself up to get the paper and pen, still clenching the dagger in my hand when suddenly I felt what appeared to be an open palm on my chest pushing me backwards on the bed. I immediately heard a male voice firmly saying: "My grace is sufficient for you. My grace is sufficient for you. My grace is sufficient for you."

After hearing the voice the third time I started trembling, wondering who was it I just heard. I even thought the voice might have been my granddad but when I called out his name there was no reply. I was now frightened and trembling and the dagger fell from my hand, as I felt physically weak. It felt like a presence had entered the bedroom and I started to cry uncontrollably. Well, that was more like bawling. I just could not stop crying.

Just as I started to compose myself, about what seemed like an hour or so later, I heard the real voice of my granddad calling me. "Annie! Annie!" He called out. But he could not hear my weak and croaking voice responding. By then I had almost lost my voice. So I had to put on a brave face and dry the tears and go round the front to see my grandpa. He thought I was having the flu but I simply told him I was not feeling very well. I could not tell him what I was up to just an hour or so before.

Can you imagine the shock I had when a few weeks afterwards while reading the Bible, I stumbled on the same words I heard in my room that day–"My grace is sufficient for you." (2 Cor 12:9). It was a shock to me because at the time I did not even know those words were in the Bible. When I found it I read the entire chapter, 2 Corinthians 12. Then my suspicion was confirmed. The voice I heard that day had to be the voice of God. Thank you Jesus! I now realise that was a supernatural intervention which saved my life that day.

Praise God!

Not long after this supernatural intervention of the Holy Spirit the Lord used me, yes me, who previously attempted to take my own life, to make a difference in the life of a lady in our church. This miracle stemmed from the good old days of 'Feet Washing' services.

God Used Me to Make a Difference – Healing Miracle from a Feet Washing service

This testimony goes back to the good old 'feet washing' service days. It is unfortunate that as I recall this testimony not many young people today would be able to relate **to it** because the Church of God on the whole no longer practices 'feet washing' as it did 'back in the day'. After what could be regarded as a negative situation it is amazing how God choses the foolish and base things of life to confound the wise. (1 Corinthians 1:27)

Each feet washing service in our church at the time I found myself having to wash the feet of a dear lady with a very unpleasant sore. Somehow it tended to always fall to me. I often wondered whether it was because I was the youngest among them. I would never know. Regardless of the reason, I did it anyway but one day I got tired of the smell. It was very unpleasant. So I prayed to the Lord a very simple prayer that night. Not just for me who had to face it once a month but on behalf of the lady who had to live with this sore every day.

During that 'feet washing' service I prayed a honest simple prayer: "Dear Father in heaven, I am tired of washing this stinking foot, so please, please heal this lady so she can continue with her life normally. And when she comes back her foot would no longer smell. Amen." I had no idea how God was going to do it but I believed that God would do it. This dear lady was a very good baker and this sore was impacting her livelihood negatively.

No long afterwards she came back to thank me for my prayers and to let me know how God had intervened to heal her. She had an operation to remove the 'rotten flesh'. Since then the sore which she had had since in her teens (over 30 years) was gone. She was the happiest I have ever seen her. Her business expanded after that. Even now she talks about her miraculous healing, the power of God shown from a simple prayer at a 'feet washing' service. A base thing maybe. God is no respector of persons, teenager or adult. He hears and answers an honest and sincere prayer regardless who you are. To God be all the glory!

Chapter Seven

Dreams And Visions!

As a young girl I started having dreams that came to pass in reality some-what literally. My mother thinks I have a gift and sometimes referred to me as a peculiar child'. One such dream was about my older brother, Tony. At the time he was a motorcyclist. I dreamt he was hit from his bike and that he injured his forehead, left elbow and knee. When I shared the dream with him in the morning, he just cuddled me and told me that I must have had him on my mind or that I must have had something to eat late that night before going to bed. I did not know about that! So I just did what I knew best, I just prayed.

Later the same day I told him of the dream, something remarkable happened. We were attending a Youth Retreat which was led by my brother Tony, who was then the Youth Director. In the afternoon he left the retreat ground to retrieve something he had forgotten at home in Golden River. When he did not return at the time expected we began to get anxious. In those days there were no mobile phones, so we had no means of knowing his whereabouts except via word of mouth and eye witness. As two of the church members were getting ready to go in search for my brother, they were stopped at the gate by a lady driving him to the hospital. He was covered in blood. He was hit from his motorcycle by her car and he suffered injuries to several areas of his body. Afterwards we found out that his injuries were just like I saw in the dream. This was remarkable!

On his return from the hospital he said to me "That dream Annie, wow! It was spot on. I will never take anything you say to me for granted ever again."

Not only was I having dreams with special meanings, the Lord has used visions to show me things that were about to happen as well. God be praised for His gifting! On these two occasions I will be sharing, I was in church when I saw these visions. The first time I got a vision was in my teenage years. Naïve and not fully understanding what was happening, God used my pastor to interpret my vision. We all lived to see the vision came to pass in our local church not long after.

The second vision I recalled then was again explained to me by my pastor. It was during one of our worship services that I saw the front door of our church opened and a mighty rush of crystal clear water rushed through and exited the back door. Over and above the rushing sound of the water I heard an audible inner voice saying to me '1 Corinthians 13'. This was repeated three times. Unsure of what to do and what had just taken place, I felt the urge to write a note to the pastor explaining the voice I had just heard. To my surprise he paused and read it. (A note from a child) I expected him to read the scripture but instead he called me up to read it and to explain to the church what I had just seen.

Nervously I went up before the congregation and began reading "Though I speak with the tongues of men and of angels and have not charity; I am become a sounding brass or a tinkling cymbal." (KJV) This was the first time I realised that 1 Corinthians 13 was called the 'Love Chapter'. Then I proceeded to tell the church about the water I had just seen gushing through the front door and then through the building, and out through the back door. Our pastor then interpreted the vision to mean that God was cleansing the church and that lots of blessings will follow. For example, the backsliders (members who have left the church for one reason or other) will return and new people will come to know the Lord. He emphasised the importance of us showing genuine love to one another before any of this could happen.

Surely we witnessed God turning our local church around and we experienced an exponential growth in membership in a reasonably short time. Within three years the membership grew from 6 to 33. Our local church was presented with a plaque at the National Convention in recognition of our growth. Yes, lots of backsliders did return just like the pastor had said. The community too was boosted and with help from the Member of Parliament a community youth club was formed with some of the church members were placed in leadership positions there. So the blessings did follow. Pastor often reminded me of the vision and the interpretation. That was an encouragement to me and made me realise that God does speak to people in different ways. To God be the glory.

Another Vision

In another vision the Lord showed me I was also in church, as an adult. During the Sunday service I saw my mother running from my big brother and hiding behind the front door from a missile he threw at her. I was living in Kingston at the time and my relatives lived about 25 miles away in St Catherine. Although the service was near to its closure, I just could not wait until the final prayer; I asked the person in charge if they could pray immediately for my mother. And she did it right away, no question asked. Praise God for Godly leaders! It was remarkable how timely that prayer was. I was to find out later that it saved my mother's life–just at the particular time. In fact the Lord gave me a testimony to share when I returned to church later that evening.

As soon as I got home from church–not yet knowing what exactly had happened–I ran to make a phone call to my Mum. Then simultaneously the phone rang. I quickly picked it up and it was my sister on the line. She said "Annie, Mark (not my brother's real name) and his girlfriend nearly kill Mama up here today." She explained how he threw a stone at her which landed in the front door. When I enquired about the time this happened. It was right about the time I saw the vision and asked the brethren to pray for my Mum. When I think that God showed me Mum, the missile, and the front door exactly, I can't help but exclaim: "God is amazing!!!"

I also bless the Lord for the evangelist who did not hesitate to stop the order of service to pray because I believe that timely prayer saved my mother's life. I am not suggesting for once that I am any super woman but I know that God chooses people to carry out his purpose here on earth and once you are at the place of right standing with God He will use you, no matter what age or stage you are.

There have been many other visions I have seen and witnessed them coming to pass. I know they are visions because I sat in church and just saw the events unfold. You heard me right. No, I was not asleep. Even while living here in the United Kingdom the Holy Spirit has continued showing me various things. Some have come to pass and others are yet come to pass. My challenge is to find a mature Christian who is able to understand and interpret the visions as my pastor did in the past. I guess it is a part of my maturing process where I have no choice but to depend on the Holy Spirit, my Master Teacher, to bring clear understanding of these visions to me. It is amazing what God has done and continues to do!

Another challenge I face in the area of visions is what to do with them. I often keep silent about them and watch them unfold. However, other times I would feel a strong urge to share, but I have to be careful about this. Unfortunately, finding a spiritual mentor or a person to come alongside me in the UK has been difficult for me for some years now. As a result, I have had to live on my knees – what I call 'Prayer City'. I believe my mentor is out there somewhere. God is making the link.

Chapter Eight

Testimonies From Jamaica (Adult)

***

*SHORT CELEBRITY STATUS ENJOYED
*YOUTH CAMP MIRACLES 1 AND 2
- MY FIRST ENCOUNTER WITH THE DEMONIC INFLUENCED
- THE MISSING CAMPER–AVERTING SUICIDE THROUGH PRAYER

SHORT CELEBRITY STATUS ENJOYED

*A*s an adult I experienced what could be referred to as 'my gifting making room for me'. I was very willing to help where there was a need and at my school that willingness was sometimes misused and even abused. However, there are some things that were meant to be despite the pain and hardships faced. Now, as a budding sign language interpreter I was asked to substitute for another person at a weekend event.

Initially, I was not so happy to accept because I felt I was being used to attend events for which no payment was given while others would be selected to do events which involved payments. In fact, I only knew this because it was bought to my attention by a member of the senior leaders. She advised me not to let people in leadership 'use me.' However, on hearing of this often missed opportunity, for the first time I asked whether there was a payment involved and was told there was. I obliged; whether or not there was money involved it would not have made any difference to me anyway.

This was to be the start of something great in my life which led to me having a short stint at 'celebrity status' at the time. It was a National Heroes Day celebration in which I was asked to interpret for the Governor General of Jamaica, Sir Howard Cooke. May I point out that I only found this out when I arrived at the venue. The long and short of the story is that the Governor General being clearly impressed with my level of signing performance and the responses from the deaf audience, he recommended that I sign for the Prime Time News on our national television station – Jamaica Broadcasting Co-operation (JBC).

I was astounded when I received the call from the television station's programming department explaining that the Governor General of Jamaica, Sir Howard Cooke, had offered to patronise the programme through the Combined Disabilities Association (CDA) on television and requested that I sign as part of the programme. They told me how he described me as 'the little lady that signs smoothly'. He did not even know my name. But because I was the one that signed for him at the Heroes Day event in Spanish Town that day, he was certain about whom he spoke.

Overcome with shock and disbelief, and being the shy person I was, I asked another person I believed to be more advanced in signing than myself to attend the audition. But they came back and said the station insisted that I must attend, as the Governor General had specifically requested that I, 'the little lady that signs smoothly' be the interpreter. So after shying away from the camera on two consecutive occasions, I finally attended the audition. Believe me, it was a great experience and was soon told that I was successful.

So a few short months afterwards I, along with one of my sign language teachers started a three months trial contract at the television station to work with the Prime Time News Team. That contract went from three months to six months. Six months turned into a year and one year into two. We actually ended up interpreting for the national television station for three and a half years under the patronage of the GG. I could not have envisioned this happening to me.

From television, I gained status as an interpreter and was honoured to be asked to interpret for the then Prime Minister, Rt Hon P J Patterson, the ministry of justice and other prominent figures in our country, including Ambassador Courtney Walsh. I am grateful for organisations like the Jamaica Association for the Deaf and the Combined Disability Association which facilitated me and my gifting. My celebrity status also meant I was sought after to interpret at events like graduations and other events.

One of the most rewarding events, not in terms of money only, was the time I was one of three interpreters invited to the Jamaican House of Parliament on its historical Joint Sitting of the House of Parliament. This meant that the two leading political parties at the time – The People's National Party and the Jamaica Labour Party met for a joint sitting. I was in awe to get first hand climses of these public officials so close to me. It felt a bit like the 'stuff that dreams are made of.'

These experiences gave me the chance to reminisce and what I found was that although I was only asked initially to give my service as a substitute, (to work for the National Heroes Day event on the weekend, the officials were unknown to me at the time) there was a greater plan. Years later I realised God had a bigger and better plan for me. Not only was I paid for that one off event but an opportunity was opened up to me that not only astounded me but brought me face to face with such people I otherwise would not have been near. Much like what Proverbs 16:18 says "*A man's gift makes room for him,* And brings him before great men. (NKJV). It all makes sense now!

Remarkably, it makes sense to me now. As a teenager I had a vision of my name running among the credits on a television screen. This vision came after one of my English teachers convinced me to start liking my name. You see in those days, while living in the rural area, I think they took no pride in how they pronounce people's names. This used to annoy me. Very often I have had to take the trouble to correct the pronunciation given to my name. Instead of 'Jane' I was often called 'Djain'. Sometimes I would tell them my full name hoping this would help; but to no avail.

Therefore for many years I was determined to change my name. I could not wait for my sixteenth birthday. Until that day when my English teacher overheard me saying to someone 'I can't wait to change my name.' She called me over and asked me about it. She wanted to know what could have led me to that decision. I shared with her my desire and the reason I wanted to change my name. She then called my name a few times and how beautiful that sounded to me. I thought to myself 'if only I could hear my name being called like that more often'. My teacher managed to convince me that day not to change my name and she told me how beautiful my name was and that it was unique. She even advised me to write it down five times and say it out loud each time I wrote it.

Somehow my English teacher managed to convince me and I started liking my name again since then. Small wonder therefore, that a few weeks later I happen to envision my name running among the credits on a television screen in 'a vision'. I had no idea it was a vision at the time. In fact it did not mean anything much to me at the time. It appeared to be like a quick glimpse of a television screen that flashed in front of me with my name on it. Interestingly, at the time I was not even engaged in anything television related, and had no inclination to anyway.

However, it was during one of my first open caption TV news presentation that I remembered what I had seen in 'the vision' several years prior. When I observed the credits running on the screen and saw my name there, the vision came back vividly to my mind. Then I was able to conclude that what I had seen those years before was indeed 'a vision'. How it all panned out was simply remarkable. It all makes sense now!

YOUTH CAMP MIRACLE #1
*MY FIRST ENCOUNTER OF A DEMONIC INFLUENCE

In my adult years I continue to experience miracles from God. It was clear that the power of God was upon my life. I recall two such experiences while serving in our National Youth Camp. Several remarkable things happened of which I would like to share two.

I attended and served in my first youth camp during my penultimate year in college. I was training to become a teacher at the Mico College, now Mico University College. This experience has never left my mind as it was so dramatic it is as if it happened only yesterday.

Seeing someone operating under the 'influence' of evil spirits as David Prince puts it, was a first for me. By the way, I almost say a 'demon possessed' Christian; I know better now. The situation was that one of my dorm members and counselee (whom I will call Dainty) has been very rebellious during the first 3 days of the 5-day youth camp. This young lady had no idea that God had very big plans for her life and that her years of rebellion was about to end. At this time it did not make sense to me then. But as the night progressed, as you shall see shortly, IT ALL BEGAN TO MAKE SENSE!

During our mid-week evening service all campers were asked to come up and queue to walk under the human arch made by the camp staff. This was some-what like a bridal procession. Not surprisingly 'my trou-bled-camper' refused to go. Despite my encouraging and chiding, Dainty still refused to budge. So, as her counsellor, I told her that I will be leaving her for a while and if she changes her mind then she could come and join me and the other campers.

A few minutes after I joined hand with a fellow camp staff in the arch, Dainty approached with both her hands cupped over her ears. She sprinted throughout the length of the arch and then back to her seat. On arriving at her seat she started making some weird noises and throwing fists at everyone in her reach. Some of the elders, (all 6 feet and above) tried to restrain her but she proved to be too powerful; she broke loose from them, jumped in the air and landed heavily on the floor. I honestly thought she might have broken something because of how heavily she fell. Thankfully, that was not the case. Physically she was alright. However, more funny noises were oozing from her. Her countenance had changed and she looked wild and dangerous.

Soon afterwards one of the ministers came to me and asked me to join the deliverance team that was working with her; as she had begun using the 'deaf language' which was not known to any of them there (Sign Language). You see I am a teacher of the Deaf (TOD) but despite my having the skills in that area I was a novice to 'demons and deliverance from them'. So I knew I had to trust God fully on this assignment as it was my first experience of seeing somebody in this state. Nervous and trembling and a bit sceptical – I must add, I went to see what was happening with my 'troubled-camper, Dainty. To my surprise, she sprang towards me with her fingers clawed like a large bird going after its prey. I was frightened! I mean, I was terrified. I certainly did not expect this. When I see my dorm member and counselee lying on the floor, I could not recognise her – her countenance seemed to have completely changed. She looked different.

I quickly prayed a prayer and asked God for His coverage, His peace and His direction. I confess to you today, I was so afraid I felt my body trembling uncontrollably. Hence my insatiable need to pray for God's guidance. Then I noticed she was signing away at every question she was being asked by the Bishop and ministers and people were guessing what she meant. The ministers saw the need to call me over to help them to interpret what Dainty was signing. I was shocked to see her signing, not speaking as she was used to doing. But I just thought we had something in common here–she knew Sign Language as well. (Later I found out, to my surprise, this was to be far from the truth. She did not know Sign Language at all). It was just wishful thinking on my part.

So I began by signing to her "The blood of Jesus" and she or rather the spirit in her started to laugh uncontrollably. I then signed what the Bishop was saying to her "You are defeated Satan" and she responded in a baby-like and joking voice "Not defeated. Heh! Heh! Heh! Not defeated!" Each time the Bishop would say 'Satan, you are defeated' the spirit manifesting itself in her would always respond with those same words repeatedly – as if jeering the Bishop. When Dainty got back to signing again. I interpreted what she was signing back to Bishop Daley and he gave us instructions as to what to do in response. This went on for several minutes until she signed in an aggressive manner:

"I need to wash my face"

The Bishop then told us to use our copies of the Holy Bible to slap her gently. 'Strange,' I thought, but we all obeyed and did just what we were asked.

Prior to Bishop Daley's instruction one of the ministers sent to get water to wash Dainty's face as she had requested. But the Bishop stopped her instantly. He said:

"We will not provide any water but just slightly slap her with our Bibles. We must not give the devil what he wants."

I found that statement quite remarkable; I had never heard or thought of that before.

As soon as the first copy of the Holy Bible touched Dainty she screamed, again in a babbling voice:

"Burrn! Burrn! Burrn!" and she signed "It's Hot, it's hot!"

However, Bishop Daley advised us camp staff to continue touching her gently with the copies of the Holy Bible. And he did emphasise 'gently'. All this time she stood motionless but shut her eyes tightly. Then the bishop commanded the demons to leave her body in the name of Jesus. After what seems like forever, Dainty burst out crying. She cried uncontrollably for about 10 minutes and then suddenly she began to wash her face with the tears, nose and mouth water that were streaming from her face. At the sight of tears we were told to stop hitting her with the Bibles but just to rest them all over her body – covering her from head to feet. Her tears kept flowing and she kept on washing her face with it. Then suddenly she screamed on the top of her voice:

"JE-SUS, JESUS!!!"

This time it was her real voice – no longer babbling. Remarkably, what happened next grabbed our attention. As she called on the name of 'Jesus' we all instantly noticed a huge difference in her countenance. It was as if someone had shone a bright light in her face. She then spontaneously shouted:

"Jesus, Lord, help me!"

As she asked Jesus to help her, we (the camp staff and ministers) prayed for her. She was changed – completely transformed before our very eyes. She has not been the same since.

Dainty's face then shone like a light was shining on her. She looked around her somewhat confused. She then turned to me and asked:

"Miss, where am I?"

I told her that she was at youth camp in Clarendon. She then said to me:

"Miss, I am tired and hungry."

Then she began to explain how she felt that she had been on a long journey with some people. I thought to myself 'Well you did put up a fight with all these men who are over 6 feet tall, (the Bishop and the security personnel) and the rest of us, so I understand you would be physically tired'.

Yet another strange thing happened after Dainty was delivered. During my ensuing conversation with her, I made a discovery. As a teacher of the deaf (TOD) her Sign Language skills undoubtedly intrigued me. But when I asked her where she had learned Sign Language she turned to me and asked me:

"What is that, Miss? Sign Language, what's that?"

It was then that I realised she had not the slightest clue as to what she was doing when she signed all these 'proper signs' to us earlier. It was as though she could not hear during the time the demons were speaking through her. At one point she had even appeared blind as well. I remembered putting my hand close to her eyes and she did not even blink. Not only me but our Bishop did the same thing and she did not respond. It was as if she was not seeing anything at that point. This is all still a mystery to me because if she does not even know Sign Language how was she able to do those signs so precisely and meaningfully? How could she even respond to my signed language with such accurate signs? She used absolutely no voice. Amazing! I just have to say 'It's amazing'!

The surprises or shall I say amazement for that night was still not over. Soon afterwards we got Dainty some food. As she sat in the auditorium eating we were surprised by the shouts and breathless appearance of a man carrying a torch. One of the security officers on duty at the school had reported an incident to our security personnel at the camp. So he came running into the auditorium with his torch still on saying that some chickens in the nearby coop were flying up and dying. This suddenly reminded me of the account in Mark 5 when Jesus cast out the legion of demons from the man in the graveyard and they went into the pigs, who then ran into the sea and drowned. This was an experience I will never ever forget. God still works miracles, folks! God still works miracles today.

I hasten to add that my once 'troubled camper' Dainty was transformed from that day. For the rest of that camp a more lovely, helpful, responsive and kind camper a counsellor could not desire. She was even awarded the Most Improved Camper – my nomination, of course, supported by a wide range of both camp staff and campers. To God be the glory! On her arrival home I was reliably informed that this transformation was immediately noticeable at home as well. Thank you, Lord!

The following miracle also happened at youth camp.

YOUTH CAMP MIRACLE #2
*THE MISSING CAMPER – AFTER
INCARCERATION

A couple years later I served in Senior Youth Camp as a Prayer Co-ordinator. This was my first year serving the seniors campers. I was now married and had a daughter, Janel. During the last night service of the camp (Saturday) something remarkable happened and I would like to record this experience as well. God is indeed gracious.

All camp staff were asked to pray for the campers who had gathered at the altar that night. As I passed by this young man wearing a black and white striped shirt, the Holy Spirit spoke to me to put my hand around him and hug him 'just like I would hug my hubby'. It felt strange and weird; how do I do that and to a perfect stranger as well. So after a bit of delay and questioning–I obeyed. As I got close to the young man I heard myself whispering to him:

"Jesus loves you and I love you too".

Where did that come from? Even I was stunned because I had not thought about what I was going to say to him. I thought–it must be from the Holy Spirit. Well, I've never seen this man before, so it had to be the Holy Spirit speaking to and through me.

As I was very close to this guy I could noticed some scars on his face and he looked rather rough (not refined). Certainly not someone you would easily go up to; let alone give a cuddle to. I am just being honest here. All of that were enough to put me off, but I was convinced that this was the Holy Spirit directing me to do this. So I just had to do what I was instructed to do. I could not hold myself back.

The following morning–the final day of camp, we were all gathering our belongings and taking contact details–getting ready to return to our various parts of the country. But what happened next certainly stunned every one. Very early that morning an alarm was made that one of our campers had gone missing. After a long and frantic search the camper was found by the security team in a tree with a piece of string around his neck. He was frightened and crying: "I just could not do it, I kept hearing the little lady's voice saying Jesus loves me and she loves me too. I just could not do it!"

After he was brought back to the office he told the counsellors that he dreaded to return home. He revealed that he had been incarcerated for 8 years for murder and was out on parole. He told them that the whistle reminded him of his incarceration and could not bear to hear the final whistle blown on the camp site. He also reported that he felt such love at the camp that he dreaded returning home to the emptiness and dread. In order to get away from it all, he decided to end it all that morning.

However, on his first attempt to swing to his death he kept hearing 'the little lady's' voice speaking to him. Nobody knew who that 'little lady' was. After some help by the professionals on site he was transported to the hospital. During this time a fellow counsellor and camp secretary came to see me in my room. They were of the opinion that based on the description given by this young man, the 'little lady' whom he spoke about could have been me.

Well, I remembered speaking to many young men and women that night so it could have been any one. But when the counsellor repeated the words that he said the camper had said to him, then the pin dropped. At this point I knew it was definitely me. I remembered my saying those exact words to him the night before because they came as a surprise to me too. "Jesus loves you and I love too."

So, yes, it was me. The Lord used an unusual or more like weird instruction to prove my obedience and ultimately used my obedience to save a young man's life. Believe me, this instruction did seem weird to me as I am not known to get that close to a member of the opposite sex except for my husband. Also, and very importantly, given our culture in Jamaica, we are known for greeting with hand shakes, not embraces. So I was convinced that this was God at work supernaturally. Wow! God is good and to Him I give all the glory, honour and praise.

Chapter Nine

Testimony Time From Jamaica Cont'd

*MICO COLLEGE ENTRY FEE MIRACLE
*ANOTHER COLLEGE MIRACLE–LOVE

Both the testimonies which follow have connections with the Mico Teachers College in Kingston. They both highlight answer to prayers and God's divine provision.

God is truly a prayer-answering God. I have proven him over and over again. Let me emphasize here that our God is concerned with the big things in our lives, just as much as He is with the tiny things which we often deem insignificant. My testimonies about God's provision are many but for this book I will share two divine interventions from the distant past (in Jamaica) and a couple from this era and region (in the UK).

God deserves our praises and for years I pondered about a forum to tell others of the goodness of the Lord. Testimony time in church is far too limited. As a result I turned to expressing my thoughts and testimonies through 'journal writing' which I have been doing since the year 2000. I still do it occasionally – not as regularly as before given my busy lifestyle.

Writing my testimony is my way of saying 'thanks to God in the 'great congregation' as David puts in Psalm 35:18; and 'praise Him among much people'. Also it reminds me of God's goodness to me in order to strengthen my faith. God is truly amazing! I can't help but share about His goodness. It is my hope they will be a blessing to you.

My Mico Teachers' College Entry Fee Miracle

The incident I wish to share happened over 25 years ago but it is still very clear in my mind. Towards the end of the first term into my studies as a teacher in training, I found myself needing a miracle. I was among a group of students whose fees were in arrears. The college principal threatened to 'name and shame' us the following week in our General Assembly. His words to us were: "How can you be training to be teachers and you are not honouring your obligation to pay your fees?"

He scoulded, "That is cheating! And we are not training thieves."

Knowing I never had any intention of cheating the College out of its funding wasn't hard to fathom, but more daunting was the fact that I had no clue where that money would come from at such short notice. I wished we had more time. One thing I dreaded was being embarrassed before the General Assembly of over 500 people. So I set about praying with 'child-like faith'. So I prayed one of the most honest and simplistic prayer I could ever pray.

I knelt at the side of my little 'single bed' in my dorm that evening. I said to Abba Father:

"Dear Lord and my Father in heaven, I come to you in the name of Jesus my Saviour. Our Principal, Mr R A Shirley will be calling out the names of all who own balances on their fees next week Monday and Lord, I do not want to be one of them. I am your child, a representative of yours, so please keep me from this embarrassment. Amen"

I did not know how God was going to do this. That was not my concern anyway. I was confident however that He could do it, and do it He did! Later that same week I got a call from Miss Joyce, the lady with whom I boarded before enrolling in college. She told me that there was a 'registered mail' at the post office for me. When I enquired who the sender was, it was my uncle

Rupert from Rochester, New York, whom I had not seen nor heard from in over 16 years. The college driver offered to take me to pick up this letter and also to identify me. You have got to to believe this. To my surprise the letter had US$650 enclosed. I was shocked! Then came the tears – I just could not hold them back. Then I screamed "God, You did it! You did it!" You do not begin to know the relief I felt that day.

This was indeed a miracle. The money was enough to pay the balance of my fees for the entire year and with extra to spear. I even offered the driver 'a drink'. From the time of receiving the call to depositing the funds into the college's account was a total of 2 days but the essential issue here was that the fees were paid ahead of time prior to Monday's General Assembly – the day of 'naming and shaming'. Then I remembered the prayer I had prayed: "Lord, I am your child; I do not want to be embarrassed next Monday." I did not know how God was going to do it but I just knew He would. And He did.

As I sat in the General Assembly the following Monday morning, and listened to the names being read out, I did feel sorry for the other students, but I was so glad that I was not on that list, especially as a representative of Christ. God did it!

This was truly a miracle; given how it was that I came to receive this money. Now, my uncle had travelled to

Jamaica some time before and enquired about me. (When he left Jamaica 16 years prior I was a small child). He was given my address but when he got there I had moved to live at the college's hostel. As he had little time to see me before returning to New York, he decided to take my address and write to me instead. He had also learned that I had gone to college so he sent the money for me. As all of this happened without my knowledge; I see this provision as a timely miracle and an answer to my simple but sincere prayer by my bed-side that evening. And the timing was spot on.

Thank you Lord!

God answers prayers believers! And essentially, God is always on time!

The next miracle I will share also show how God is always on time.

ANOTHER COLLEGE MIRACLE–LOVE

Another miracle I wish to share ends with love as a by-product. Towards the end of one particular summer term, the University and Colleges Christian Fellowship (UCCF) of which I was an active member, embarked on a 'one week Prayer and Fasting'. And what were we praying for? Men. Yes, your heard I right. You see, the Christian fellowships across campus had so many men attached to them (The Adventist Fraternity and the

Apostolics) with the exception of UCCF. The fact is that their ladies had more than enough men to escort and sufficiently protect them as they walk the mile and a half journey to the Ladies Hostel after their night meetings. Unfortunately our ladies had to walk in groups of six or more with two or so men to escort us. So there was a need. We collectively believed that prayer and fasting was the way this situation would change.

To our surprise, when we returned to college after the summer break we witnessed a visible answer to prayer. That year the UCCF was graced with the presence of nine new men of God. Yes, nine! I was tasked to mentor those who belonged to the Church of God. These men were serious about their mission and vision for the Christian arm of our college. Remarkably, these nine men became life-long friends and even though they are living in different countries, today they still have a special bonding. This is truly a miracle.

Another miracle from this 'answer to prayer and fasting' mission was that one of those men, Linton, turned out to be my life-long friend, my husband and the father of our three children today. 'Husband' was never on our minds when we first decided to pray and fast for these men, well not on my mind for sure. Those days it was like I had blinkers on when it came to relationships. I was so focussed on my education; I probably missed signs directed at me. However, it was amazing how two years after I left Teachers' College we met again at a bus stop and this began a journey for us; and the rest is history. Needless to say, God does answer prayers and gives 'extras' sometimes. Indeed, **it all makes sense now!**

Chapter Ten

* Powerful Healing Miracles From Our Staff Room

TOOT

*THE POWER OF FORGIVENESS (ADULT)
*OUR BABY MIRACLE
*ONE KIND ACT WITH RIPPLE EFFECTS

*A*s I recall yet another mighty work of God, it still encourages me today as it did then. Just know that timing is important to God. He is always on time! Not often do we see instant healing miracles but God allowed me to see this on a triple scale, at my place of work. We cannot seem to make sense of many of the things we go through while we are going through them. But after a while, in retrospect, it all makes sense now!

Not very long after I started a Prayer Meeting group at my work place, God showed up in a remarkable way. This particular morning our meeting was being led by a young lady who was not a practising Christian but a believer (Pauline). Towards the end of the prayer meeting she asked me to pray. During that prayer, the Holy Spirit led me to pray for the three members of staff who were critically ill at the time and obviously away from work; all were on sick leave. One lady, (Mrs P), had stage 4 bone cancer which had spread throughout her body. Another (Miss A) had had an open heart surgery and the other (Miss B) had a serious mental illness and was still hospitalised. Mrs H and Miss M were sent home to recuperate but unfortunately, Mrs P was told there was nothing else that the doctors could do for her. She was literally sent home to die.

As the presence of the Lord was so real and powerful in the staff room that morning, I found myself walking on my knees – I was too weak to stand up. I could her myself calling out the names of my three co-workers. As I called the name of the third lady, I realised I was no longer praying in English – I was praying in an unknown language and for a considerable time. This was a 'first' for me – (I have never had this happen to me before). As soon as I said 'Amen' I witnessed streams of smoke leaving my mouth and going out into the atmosphere. Believe me, I was frightened. Because I had been feeling a burning sensation in my tummy since I called the names of the three ladies in my prayer. Hmmm! Strange. What was that all about? I had no clue.

Any way I finished praying and sat down quietly to listen to what God was saying to us. I felt the Lord saying to us 'to wait'. All day long my body was under such anointing I just can't explain it. Now, because I had no clue as to what the 'burning sensation and 'the smoke' meant, I decided to speak to my pastor and spiritual mentor, Rev Novel G Wilson, to see if he could shed some light on it.. (My husband was his associate pastor at the time). So later on that day I called my senior pastor, Rev Wilson, and told him what I had experienced that day. He listened carefully. Then he explained to me that the burning sensation represented the fire and passion of the Holy Spirit and that the smoke I saw was just a physical manifestation that virtue had left my body to those people I had been praying for. What he said next grabbed my attention instantly. He said to me "Sis Jane, expect a miracle, my sister!"

I had no idea how long I was to wait to expect a miracle but God brought the evidence of supernatural healing the very next day. On my way to school the following morning I felt a presence sitting on the hood of my car. Then the car started to shake violently. I had to grab the steering wheel firmly as I was really struggling to control my usually comfortable Toyota Camry Luminere. So I did what I knew best, I prayed in the name of Jesus. In fact I called on the name of Jesus seven times and on the seventh time, amazingly the car settled down, running smoothly as before. Wow! This made no sense to me at all. But on arrival at school half an hour later, (safely, Thank God!) I was to realise what that was all about. **'It all makes sense now!'**

As I entered the staff room I was greeted by Miss A, the lady who had the open heart surgery. Feeling so glad to see her I rushed to greet her and to give her a big 'tender' hug. She was all smiles. She then said to me

"I came to school this morning to ask you one thing, Jane. Does your church believe in speaking in tongues?"

To which I answered in the affirmative. Then I asked her why is that important?

What she said next surprised me. She responded:

"You see, yesterday at about 8:35a.m I was at home dying. I went to use the ladies' room so while I was in the bathroom and about to give up on life, I heard your voice, Jane, coming through my bathroom window, speaking in tongues. And when I heard your voice I felt a warm sensation which entered me from my head down to my heart and then down to my feet. Then I suddenly shook and felt alive again. That's why I am here today."

I quickly grabbed a seat. Suddenly the explanation about the 'heat and smoke' my senior pastor gave me the day before started to 'make sense now'. Then some of the teachers who overheard the prayer I prayed the day before stared to explain to Miss M what had happened. Miss M then asked us about the time at which this prayer was being made. When she heard the time, she agreed that it was the exact same time she was 'dying'. Everybody just burst out praising God for this miracle.

While the teachers were rejoicing with Miss A, our principal (referred to as 'head teacher' here in the UK) interrupted. We all thought she was coming to shut us up and move us along. But instead she had another praise report of a healing miracle. This time it was about Mrs P (the lady with the incurable bone cancer). Mrs P's son had just been on the phone with our principal. He reported that his mother has had an experience that was unbelievable. He told her that about 8:35 a.m. yesterday his mother laid on her bed, dying. He was standing over her bed at the time thinking any number of things at that moment when suddenly she started shaking and speaking. His mother had told him that she felt a heat ran through her body like electricity and that she felt strength came back into her dying body. He said he witnessed it all – the change in her countenance and hearing her speak intelligibly again. She even told him that she felt like she could come back into work real soon.

Our principal did explain to Miss P's son that at that exact time yesterday, prayer was being made on the behalf of his mother and that she believes his mother had just received a miracle. The young man had no choice than to admit that his mother did receive a miracle right before his unbelieving eyes. So once again this 'heat and smoke' which made no sense to me at the time, was beginning to 'make sense to me now!' To God be all the glory!

Wasn't our principal glad to see Miss A that morning? That is an understatement. And in addition, for her to hear this promising news about Mrs P. She was overjoyed. She too joined us in praising God, like any good Baptist deaconess could. She remarked: "If ever I had any doubt that God still works miracles, I am changed today. Jane, you proved to me that God still uses people to heal today. Thank God!"

The third co-worker was not to be denied her miracle. Later that week Miss B (the lady who had mental illness) was released from the hospital. Her family got in touch with the school's principal a couple days later. God still works miracles, today. He is indeed a very present help in times of trouble. "It all makes sense now!"

This time of miracle has made history in our school. Even though there were some unbelievers in our meeting that morning, some have openly confessed Jesus as their Lord and saviour. Others have come to me privately to say that they felt the need to recommit their ways to the Lord. Some have continued to walk in their faith since then. So generally, God was being glorified on a wide scale in our school. Indeed, **it all makes sense now.**

When I mentioned my plans to migrate to England a couple years later, my fellow work colleagues challenged me to 'keep the fire burning for God.' My principal, Miss Clara Ricketts warned me: "Don't you ever change, Jane. Continue to be obedient to the voice of God and let Him use you.' Those challenges have truly humbled me and have kept me grounded when I am faced with temptations and trials here in the UK, and anywhere I go for that matter. Somewhat like the challenge my dear neighbour, Miss Myrtle, (God rest her soul) posed to me at my baptism many years ago. (See my baptism account). **IT ALL MAKES SENSE NOW!**

THE POWER OF FORGIVENESS (ADULT)

In providing a background to the mighty healing miracle of one of the ladies mentioned above – Mrs P, it makes sense to focus on the power of forgiveness. A few years earlier, when she had learnt that I was her supervisor she was not a happy bunny. She immediately remarked: 'Mi nuh want no young girl fi supervise me.' So what that meant in English was that she was not approving of me being a younger member of staff to be her supervisor. I realised I had a real challenge on my hand.

Challenges did inevitably arise. She was disrespectful to me in front of the students. My calm handling of the situations seemed to have aggravated her even more. Eventually a few weeks later she physically assaulted me. The mistake she made was that she did it in front of some of the upper year students who would not stand to a hair on my head being touched. So two of the boys spontaneously jumped to my defence and were ready to 'give it to her' with clenched fists and all. After some persuasion they managed to compose themselves. I told them emphatically – 'That's not the way we resolve conflict boys. We talk about things, not get physical.'

Thankfully they obeyed me. Not very long after this incident the same Mrs P was diagnosed with terminal bone cancer. Some people at our school had started to say things like she should not have touched the pastor's wife. However, I knew better than to feel revengeful. So my heart was set on praying for her healing, despite the horrible way she treated me in the past. Then the miraculous staff room prayer meeting happened several months later (as mentioned earlier).

Once Mrs P received her healing and she was well enough to return to work, the Lord used me to be instrumental in her life in such a way I deem it the 'power of forgiveness.' Having had some experience of 'medical boarding' this experience was very handy to me here. I did work with the Chief Medical Officer's secretary the summer before my employment as a teacher began. My job there was 'medical boarding'. So armed with this knowledge I was then able to advise the head teacher as to what to do to help Mrs P. Then as her supervisor (who she did not care to have initially) I had to fill out portions of her form as well as to guide her with the completion of her portion. Medical boarding provided financial support for her while she was away from work after sick leave has ended.

Not only was God using me to help her financially, He instructed me to drive her into work as well. To tell you the truth, I argued with the Holy Spirit about this. I even reminded the Holy Spirit that she lived off my route (as if He did not know). Then I reminded Him of the early morning traffic. However, as usual I lost the argument with the Lord, so I had to make the phone call to Mrs P.

When I asked her how she got to work she told me how much money she had to spend on taxis. She was delighted to say the least, when I offered to drive to her to and from work. She even asked me 'Will you really do that for ME?' She emphasised the 'me'. That is the power of forgiveness. By my own strength I don't know if I could do it but I trusted God to do it through me.

So here I was a few months later taking the same Mrs P into work and returning her home daily. I felt this was another example of the 'power of forgiveness'! Eventually we became best buddies at work and anything I needed she would readily offer to help. It was an extraordinary transformation. The Power of Forgiveness in action indeed!

This next miracle caused my faith to soar to an all-new high. It makes perfect sense to me now.

OUR BABY MIRACLE

One of the most transforming things our family experienced was our 'Baby Miracle.' When Linton and I were married for a year we started trying for a baby. After several failed tests and thousands of dollars being spent, we decided to get a thorough examination. I was diagnosed with hormone imbalance which according to the experts, would require me to have fertility treatments for at least twenty four months before any fertilization could be remotely possible.

The news was sad but we gladly embarked on this course of treatment, maintaining a positive outlook. At least we knew what the problem was. My gynaecologist was supportive and explained the processes I would have to go through. I was happy to try anything. Of course at this time we were determined to pray through this process. Our church members were praying for us in addition to our family members. So after just two months on the twenty-four months programme, I stood before the bathroom mirror and something dramatic happened.

As I stood with the tablets in my hand about to put them into my mouth, I found my hand stuck by my lips. It could go no further. Then I felt a comforting presence in the bathroom with me. Suddenly I felt a compulsion not to take the tablets. This was strange but I decided to put the tablets back into the bottle. As I came out of the bathroom I told my husband what had happened and he said that if I am not taking my tablets neither will he. We were both going to trust God completely on this matter. It did not make much sense then but ... it all make sense now.

Two months later, while we were on vacation in New York something remarkable happened. I found myself having food cravings which was different, especially when I started craving fried dumplings made by strangers. That was unheard of for me! But my brother-in-law kept hinting that there might be something going on with me. I failed to even entertain the idea that I could probably be pregnant. Scared maybe.

As these cravings intensified and I started feeling upset at the scent of food, I could ignore these signs no longer. Then I mustered the courage to ask them to get a pregnancy testing kit for me. Whether I would have the courage to use it was would be another matter altogether.

Since I have had so many disappointments in relation to pregnancy testing, then you can understand my apprehension. But after some time I decided to go through with it. My husband began to get nervous for me when he realised the length of time I spent in the bathroom. He became curious and started knocking. As I opened the door and he saw the tears on my face and the test kit in my hand, he immediately cuddled me and began to say how sorry he was. He explained that he can understand the disappointment I must have felt yet again.

What he did not realise was that I was crying tears of joy. You should have seen his face when I told him the test was positive. The indicator marks did confuse me at first as well because it was different from those in Jamaica. I explained to him that negative was indicated by a minus sign

(-) but positive was indicated by a double minus or an equal sign (=); not a + sign as we were used to. At this point we were both overjoyed, happy to report to our relatives of the miracle we have just witnessed. Now we knew we were never to use those fertility tablets again.

The shock was also shared by my gynaecologist. On my return to Jamaica I went to see her with the test results. To say she was shocked is an understatement. Upon seeing the kit she immediately slumped in her chair and covered her mouth in amazement. She remarked that this must be a miracle given my diagnosis and twenty-four months treatment period required. She said she will have to physically check me to be sure. And as was expected I was very pregnant – eight weeks old. This is truly answer to prayers. Our baby miracle. To God be the glory!

Remarkably, our baby miracle doubled in the same time that was assigned for my twenty-four months hormone treatment. The fact is in exactly two years to the day I was back in the labour ward giving birth to our second daughter. None of us saw this coming. God is truly amazing! God answers prayers indeed.

The next testimony is about a kind deed which I never thought would have impacted us in quite the way it has, even today.

ONE KIND ACT WITH RIPPLE EFFECTS

Prior to migrating to the UK we decided to leave our minibus with the gentleman who taught me to drive, Mr Evelyn (who has since gone to be with the Lord). We had no idea what that act of kindness was to have meant to us and our migration. It all make sense now.

When I met up with Mr Evelyn to inform him of our plan to give him our Toyota townace minibus as we were leaving for the United Kingdom, he was shocked and even commented that he had to pinch himself to see whether he was dreaming or was it reality. He was pleased because his own minibus was decaying and he would soon have to replace it and he said he could not afford a replacement at the time. But while all those were blessings for our friend, what he said to us after-wards was to bless us immensely.

As our conversation continued he asked where we were going. When he heard the town and county that we were going to, he smiled and said to us 'That was where I lived for 36 years.' Then he asked which school my husband would be working at. His smile grew bigger. He told us that that was the school that his children and grandchildren had attended. Coincidence? I don't think so.

Now following one act of kindness my family and I were to receive blessing returned to us by the same person. It is not often that you see this. Mr Evelyn was able to provide guidance to us about the town, the school and he connected us with one of his friends whom he believed would take good care of us. As a former bus driver in the UK, he even drew a map to help us to understand our route to the hotel from the London Heathrow Airport.

Mr Evelyn gave us a military award to present to his friend, Mr Cecil Harrison, who owns a business a few miles from where we were to be staying. He said as soon as he sees the award then he would instantly know who sent us. On the day following our arrival, we visited his friend and the excitement he expressed to us when he saw the military plaque was clear to see. He warmly welcomed us to the UK and told our children to call him 'Grandad'. How lovely was that? Then he proceeded to inform us that the plaque was a shared award between himself and Mr Evelyn while they served in the military.

Mr Harrison also happened to be a deacon in the Church of God in Christ (COGIC) and was happy to learn that my husband was a pastor in Jamaica. We attended his church for a few weeks until we were connected to one of our denominations. He was very instrumental in helping us with the letting agencies here and our living arrangements. At one point he advised us to leave the expensive bed-and-breakfast facility we were in. He even went as far as to ask one of his clients to help us with temporary accommodation until we got a rented property. His wife cooked and brought food to the house for us. Even today they are a dear friends of our family. Such blessings! And to know it began with one small act of kindness. It all makes sense now!

Part Two

Chapter Eleven

Testimonies In The UK

Background to coming to the UK

I will use the testimony I shared previously in another forum to give a background to my coming to live in the UK.

(The following is an excerpt from my inauguration sermon as chairman to Churches Together in Hitchin, St Mary's Parish Church on 19th January 2014 – 'My Testimony' in a sermon entitled 'Is Christ Divided?')

"Over 11 years ago I left the warmth of my country, family and friends; I left a thriving teaching and Sign Language Interpreting careers as well as a thriving ministry to accompany my husband on a trip to England where he would work as a Maths teacher. Two teaching agencies had come to Jamaica to recruit teachers for the UK and USA. So we 'bit the bait' and unbeknown to us that we would still be teaching in the UK schools after 11+ years. (We initially came for 2 years). Other than teaching, however, we realised God had other plans.

I am assured of this fact that God had other plans for us; this occasion is undoubtedly one of them. Imagine with me if you **can**, sometime in June 2002 I went to my boss's office to speak with her about my family's plan to migrate to England when she met me at the door. She said: "Jane how strange, I was just coming to see you." Curiously I enquired what she wanted to see me about (of course hoping I had not done anything wrong) but she insisted that I tell her what I was coming to see her about, first.

So I did. Her reaction was mixed–shock, despair, congratulatory and disappointment all rolled into one. Then she literally placed both her hands on her head in despair. Later my reaction was also mixed when she proceeded to inform me that she was coming to let me know that my application for Senior Teacher level 3 (next to deputy head position) had just been approved by the Ministry of Education. To make matters worse she continued:

'And it's the first time, Jane, in my 12-years' role as principal that I have seen the Ministry of Education approve an application so quickly.'

As you can well imagine, I was speechless. Friends, I had a choice to make. Do I still go to England to accompany my darling husband (like we had pledged to do before we got married – "Wherever one goes, both go") or do I just forget our 'little pledge' and just take up my new position, my new opportunity, my career expansion and let my husband go alone. Needless to say that choice is why I am here today being appointed as chair of Churches Together in Hitchin. You see, I did not even get to sit in my new office and to get the $7,000 plus Jamaican dollar (JD) extra on my salary. My position would have become effective on September 1st 2002 but insanely on August 25th I was on Air Jamaica with my husband, two infants (3 years 5 months and 1 years 5 months old), the baby sitter and 10 pieces of luggage. Who does that? I asked myself 'What am I doing?' My mother asked me, my Senior Pastor asked me, my friends and colleagues asked me. I sometimes wondered: 'did I need a check-up from my neck up?'

My only answer I could give to these people was "Purpose, maybe!" My reply has always been "I don't even know why we came. To get the experience I suppose! And as Linton puts it "This must be our Abrahamic journey, Jane" ('But at least Abraham was given clear instructions as to where to go and what to do' I would often mutter back). That same question has been asked of Linton and I on several occasions since we arrived here in England. Our response has always been the same. "I don't even know why we came here. To get experience I suppose! Our Abrahamic journey, maybe!"

What else could it be though? You see, life was good for us back home in Jamaica. Linton and I both had well-paying teaching jobs, we had two thriving congregations where Linton served as pastor for 5 years and later on as an associate pastor to Bishop Novel Wilson in Portmore for a further 2 years (Our Senior Pastor, Bishop Novel G. Wilson is still there, by the way, and with whom we continued to enjoy a great relationship as our spiritual Father).

I also did enjoy a bit of celebrity status as a National Sign Language Interpreter to various ministers of government including the reigning Prime Minister (Rt Hon P J Patterson) at the time. My skills were also employed by the Ministry of Education, the Ministry of Justice, as well as private law firms and business personnel including Miss Kathy Levy former Miss World Beauty Contest winner. This had eventually blossomed into my introduction as a Sign Language Interpreter to the nation patronised by the then Governor General, Sir Howard Cooke. I guess this is what the Bible refers to in Proverbs 18:16 'A man's gift maketh room for him, and bringeth him before great men' (KJV).

As a Sign Language Interpreter I did 'open caption' presentations next to the weekend news and sports presenters for Prime Time News at the Jamaica Broadcasting Co-operation (JBC) as it was known then; where I worked for three and a half years. A three months trial turned into six months by popular demand, then to a year, then a year turned into two years and so on. This programme was patronised by the Governor General himself and part sponsored by the Combined Disabilities Association (CDA) and the Jamaica Association for the Deaf (JAD) for whom I worked at the time.

The Big Questions then–So why would any well thinking young woman do such an irrational thing as to leave all the fame and recognition behind, to come to a place she does not know, or have any known relatives? Which well-meaning ambitious young woman does that? I really do not know why. BUT I believe God has a plan; only I did not know it then. It is certainly beginning to make more sense to me each day. My inauguration today is undoubtedly a part of His plan."

Culture Shock

Upon our arrival in the UK the culture shock experienced was instant. As we watched the aircraft's decent at the London Heathrow Airport our first observation was the brown brick buildings. Everything looked brown and grey, as far as the eyes could see. Quite a contrast to the brightly coloured and varied designs of houses in Jamaica. However I loved the uniformity in size and shape of the buildings in sight.

Not all the shocks were negative. The culture shock which I found humorous were the 'smiles.' Generally, I found the people pleasantly smiling when you approach them–with a wide smile from ear to ear. But as soon as I paused to return the sentiments I would notice that their smiles had already disappeared. These smiles were so short lived, I hardly caught one properly. Then I thought to myself 'Was that a real smile?' When I observed it happened over and over again, I realised it probably was the new country's culture to smile quickly.

Then the hotel we were told we would be staying in–upon our arrival it turned out to be a house with a 'bed and breakfast' facility. O dear! I was expecting a proper hotel like the Hilton. Very ambitious thought there. We had never been in a bed and breakfast facilities back home; so it was new to us.

The culture shocks continued. It was interesting to discover that the sign language system here in the UK was far different to the ASL system in which I was trained up to interpreter level. The 'before leaving' research done was limited. Also many things that were promised to us by the agency did not materialise in the end. However, my husband and I used the opportunity to do some leg work and we discovered much, despite the culture shocks.

We learnt to adjust to the cultural changes here and soon found ourselves fitting in as best as possible. One thing I did not do when I came to the UK was to share much about my background with the people I met, except for work related matters. My hope was that I would be welcomed and accepted as an individual rather than for what I have done in the past.

In retrospect, my decision could have been a good thing or a bad thing, given the celebrity culture that I think exists here. I just cannot be sure. But when more information about my background started to emerge several years later, there was shock and disbelief among many people we already knew. It was humbling to hear some saying to me: 'You are so humble and unassuming, no one would ever know you had so much experience even with celebrities.' For this and all other mercies I give all the honour and glory to God Almighty. It all makes sense now!

As a migrant the next testimony is probably one to which many people can relate, as it involves the Home Office. Our experiences were many and varied but it is my personal belief that a miracle, or better yet, some miracles were tied up in them.

Chapter Twelve

Charting Our Home Office Experiences

—————•⟨☉⟩•—————

*HOME OFFICE SAGA AND MIRACLE
*THE CALL OF THE DECADE
*THE CONSEQUENCE

As a family we have witnessed many occasions in which the Lord worked out our Home Office dilemmas. One short contract after another, one raise of immigration application fees after another and finally the change of immigration law which set us back 3 years. (Details will follow). These situations did not make any sense to us. All we felt was frustration after frustration.

But it truly 'makes perfect sense now' after years of reminiscing on why things happened the way they did. There were lots of questions then. Much more questions than they were answers at the time. Who? What? Where? Why? How? Often the question was 'What on earth is going on?' Or even 'What have we done to deserve this? 'What have we done wrong?'

Fortunately or unfortunately those questions could not be answered then. It is now almost eleven and a half years since our family arrived in the UK and we have only received our citizenship three years ago. Three to four years later than most of our teacher colleagues who came to England even after us. So yes, there were many questions going through our minds. But as the Lord favoured us time and time again we can finally make sense of the whole situation. It is about His timing not ours. It all makes sense now!

On arrival in England we enquired about the Home Office law governing 'leave to remain'. So were looking forward to applying for it at the end of our first three years of being in the country. One cannot image the disappointment we felt when we were told due to some change in our statuses we would need to return to Jamaica and reapply for re-entry into the country based on new regulations being imposed with immediate effect. The change of law caught us.

After much persuasion, sending and receiving correspondences, visit to our local Member of Parliament (MP), and solicitor and not to mention the expenses incurred, we finally got our prayers answered and the Home Office reneged on their original decision. We were granted leave to remain the only draw-back being our years of being in the country were literally wiped out and they started counting again from that point. We lost 3 years off our stay in the country, so we had to start counting again.

Not only that, the length of time in which work permit holders were permitted to work before applying for leave to remain had also increased from 4 to 5 years. Why then were we set back like this? More questions than answers. But we just sort of blocked the long wait from our minds and continued life as usual much like Job, we waited until our change came – 5 years later.

Bearing in mind that during that time our leave to remain would have expired and we would have had o make yet another application to Home Office prior to the end of the 5 year regulation which incurred a big chunk of our savings. Given that immigration fees had also recently gone up and that our family had now grown to 5. Our son, Joshua, was the new addition to the family – born only seven weeks prior to when this Home Office ordeal began. More details to follow in the chapter entitled Our Home Office Saga.

This was a very stressful time for me, especially so soon after giving birth. But one thing I knew then was that I only wanted to 'be in the will of God'. I was prepared to go back home to Jamaica with my young baby and two infant daughters, if that was what God wanted for us. I was to have found out later that He clearly had other plans. More about the whole ordeal in the Leave to Remain Miracle – Our Home Office Saga below.

Only now 'it makes sense' to me. During the process everything was blurred. I could only think 'Lord whatever is your will, Please Lord, let it be done.' The truth is, I was also thinking; "Lord, please let it be done quickly." Only I was not praying it out loudly to Him. However, He knew my thoughts anyway.

LEAVE TO REMAIN MIRACLE
*OUR HOME OFFICE SAGA

By the first two months of our son's birth, we were faced with what I call the 'Home Office Saga'. One day while nursing my six weeks old baby I saw my husband coming home with his brief case and laptop. I thought to myself:

"What could have made him come home so early?"

My enquiring mind could not help but wonder what was going on; as this was quite different from the norm. My husband could not get in through the back door soon enough when I blurted out to him:

"What happen? Why are you home so early?"

It was then that the 'Home Office Saga' began. My husband explained to me that his Head teacher had received a letter from the Home Office ordering her to ask him to leave the premises as he was in the country illegally.

"What?" I screamed. "How could this be?"

This message was not only a shock to me but also to both Linton and his head teacher.

He continued to explain that his head teacher had called him into her office to have discussions with him about the correspondence she had just received from the Home Office regarding his application for leave to remain. She made him aware that his application had been denied. Just then I noticed a letter that was earlier dropped through our letter box. Upon checking what the content was, it was discovered that that was his documents from the Home Office – identical to the ones sent to his employer.

So here we were faced with a dilemma. The big question is what must we do now? Clearly, we had to let the news settle then I asked him the question.

"What can we do now?

He was advised by his head teacher that she will get in touch with the Member of Parliament for Luton and discuss the situation with him. At the time our MP was Kelvin Hopkins.

It was an error on the Home Office part because Linton was never here illegally. His status was changed from Permit Holder to Dependent during our first two years. How did this come about, you may ask? And I would reply: "It's a bit complicated!"

At our second application for leave to remain in the UK my husband came up with this grand idea to apply on his own. Not with the rest of the family. The resultant implication here is firstly, Linton would no longer be my dependants but rather, if granted he will revert to being the main permit holder. The second implication was that the three children would now become my dependents – as I was recently granted a 5-years work contract, much longer than what Linton was given previously (2 years).

The Home Office has been offering Linton only short spans on his work contracts. The very first contract was granted for only 3 months. And would you believe it if I say that it was that same 3 months contract on which we travelled to the UK in the first place. Talk about step of faith here! Rather I would call it a 'leap of faith.'

Linton's first extension on his work contract was granted for one year only; then his next was for two years. Within that time the immigration laws had changed and the time to be awarded indefinite leave to remain was extended. These small contract times were very frustrating to Linton, so he thought he might be in with a chance to become the main permit holder again (thus he applied by himself) with the hope of the rest of us being his dependents afterwards. Literally going back to the way it had been when we first arrived in this country. So not long after my application for leave to remain, for myself and the two children; we received our passports back stamped with five years extension.

This Home Office saga started when upon anxiously awaiting the arrival of Linton's passport back from the Home Office, following his sole application, we were greeted with this: No work, no permit, and no leave to remain. How daunting the prospects here! One day I was home at about lunch time and noticed him walking home with his laptop bag and other belongings. I thought then that he probably was not feeling well so had to come home from school. But to my surprise that was not even near to the reality. His head teacher has had to ask him to leave the job based on a letter she received from Home Office alleging that he was in the UK illegally. That meant that he was denied the 'leave to remain' based on that premise. Because according to them 'they could not see him entering the country legally'. Really? Nothing was further from the truth. Our lives were instantly turned upside down.

However, his very supportive Head Teacher took it upon herself to immediately speak with the Member of Parliament on Linton's behalf. In the meantime she advised him to go home and that she will be doing all she can to have the situation which I now call 'the Home Office Saga' sorted. What I did not know was that a letter had come home from the Home Office and it did suggest that 'Linton had entered the country illegally.' How could this be? This clearly was a mistake. How else would we have got here in the first place? Although he clearly was disturbed by this saga, he recalled his Head Teacher saying to him that the Home Office can be difficult to deal with at times but as 'he is a man of faith' she is hoping for his sake all will work out well; as she did not have the faith. Thankfully it did. Yes, it did!

The following day Linton called to set an appointment with Mr Kelvin Hopkins (Labour) our Luton MP (still the serving MP today). He was instrumental in helping to sort out matters with the Home Office. Very soon after his letter we were contacted by them.

THE SAGA THICKENS

However, the situation still looked a bit grim though; because I had only recently resigned my job due to ill health. During a telephone conversation with the Home Office Linton mentioned this to the representative. I personally did not think, at the time, that my husband needed to say all of that to them. (Especially when I heard the consequences of this legitimate resignation). In fact, I was fuming. I thought "See what being too honest does? It punishes us." I couldn't wait for him to get off the phone to accuse him of 'saying too much'. However I suddenly felt an inner peace that God was going to work this out somehow and that His will is being done. I was even happy to go back home to Jamaica because I was missing home, friends, family and work a lot. But heh, ho! I have learnt that Jehovah has the final say on everything. That meant the Home Office rulings as well.

The Consequences seemed more than I could bear. What this resignation meant was that not only was Linton here 'illegally' but so were myself and my dependants too (the children). It also meant that my 5-year contract was now lost and my stay was now revoked. "What am I hearing?" I thought. I was literally dumb founded. After collecting my nerves I managed a question. "So what is going to happen to us now, given I didn't know that resigning meant me losing my right to remain in the country?"

To which she replied: "I will have to speak with my superiors about it. This is bigger than I previously thought. It is completely out of my hands now."

I was left with two choices – Pray for favour and wait for her response or give up hope, and go back home. I choose the former. I started interceding to the 'superior of all superiors' and believe me He did come through for me and my family.

During my time of interceding, Linton did the leg work by employing the service of a solicitor. It turned out that quite a few weeks had passed without us hearing from her. However, one fine day not long after the Home

Office representative had gone to speak with her 'superiors,' I got a call.

THE TELEPHONE CALL OF THE DECADE

The phone rang and as expected, I nervously rushed to get it. It was the Home Office calling. The lady (I won't mention her name) I spoke with before was on the line and she asked if I were sitting down. Hearing such a question, my heart sunk almost to my toes. However, I mustered some courage and sat down. I also got a pen and paper. Then she dropped the BUMBSHELL!

She proceeded to tell me that the Home Office had decided to renege on their decision, and will be returning Mr Grant (my husband) back to his former position as the permit holder and myself and the children as his dependants'. Wanting so much to hear her say it again, I asked "And what does that mean in English please Miss ...? She kindly obliged and explained again that we were now safe, as my husband is being returned to his former position as the permit holder and us as his dependents. I could not hold back the scream. I immediately shouted "Thank you Jesus!" before thanking the kind lady on the other end of the telephone line. You can well imagine the jubilation.

The jubilation did continue. In Jamaican lingo we would say 'Mi even get brawta' – translated 'I got a little extra. The Home Office representative went on to ask me about my newly born son. She asked: "You said that you have a baby, right Mrs Litchmore-Grant?" To which I responded in the affirmative. She then proceeded to offer me an endorsement paper or temporary passport for our son. She advised me to send her two passport photos of him as soon as possible so she can prepare his endorsement document just in case I wish to travel with my son. How is that for blessing on top of blessing? If only you could see my face then! I could not wait to deliver this specially 'good news' to my husband.

The Home Office representative also advised me to send her all our passports along with the photos of our baby. I told her that we had not yet received our passports from her office. It was then that we were finding out that our passports had already been sent back to our solicitor over a month before. So we now had another problem. We now had to find out from our solicitor how and why we had not been sent back our passports even after one month.

As this Home Office saga thickens, we were however pleased that we got the miracle we had been praying for. I was convinced that this hick-up too will pass. "Satan, ain't no stopping us now" I thought. Thankfully after some to-ing and fro-ing with our solicitor we finally had our passports back after a frank meeting with my husband the following day. You see, she tried to put the blame on the Home Office. She said something to the effect that they 'broke protocol' in informing us of their change of position on the matter before informing her first. She also had an issue with the fact that they had gone so far as to inform us that our passports were sent back to her over a month ago. It has been over 4 weeks and she had not even got in touch with us to tell us our fate. Unbelievable!

Linton's visit to the solicitor's office that day also revealed that we had been advised by Home Office to return to Jamaica and reapply to re-enter the UK. This was like what Jamaicans would call 'punkus pan pankas' (Translation–One trouble after another). I am so thankful we had not known about any of this verdict when we were speaking with the Home Office representative. Although she had obviously believed that we had our passports in hand, God must have kept us from this added stress in the whole process. Regardless of what this solicitor said at this stage Linton demanded our passports from her. This was to start a new process for us.

THE CONSEQUENCE

The consequence of reinstating Linton as permit holder, however, meant that the whole process had to be restarted. The almost three years we spent in the country so far could no longer hold. Therefore the Home Office would start counting our years again from this point. This meant that it will take another three years for us to qualify for application for permanent residency. It suddenly dawned on me that this was a big price we had to pay but we were more than willing to pay it. This was our cross and we were willing to bear it. As the saying goes 'Good things comes to those that wait.' So wait we did.

During my waiting I would sometimes contemplate how easy all of our fellow teacher colleagues had it, in relation to their leave to remain and permanent residency applications. Some who even came to the UK after us were granted permanent residency and citizenship before us. But I took consolation in the fact that our story is unique. We had truly identified that our story was different – this was indeed 'our cross' and we had no intention to not bear it. These experiences have made my faith stronger – I would not have had it any other way. Now we have a testimony of hope to encourage others who may find themselves in similar situations. To God be the glory!

AND THE SAGA THICKENS YET AGAIN

Although it seemed that the saga thickens again. However, after we had worked for another 3 years in preparation for application to the Home Office, to our utter surprise and horror, the immigration law changed. It now takes 2 years longer to qualify for application for permanent residency. Talk about a lengthy journey for us. OUR CROSS I guess. So what that meant for us was that we were faced with a situation in which we would now have to make yet another application for leave to remain before we could apply for permanent residency.

It must be noted here that along with the change of law, there was yet another rise in the application fees. We had already experienced a rise of application fees. This time we had to pay a sum of money for each person rather than the 'family fee' we previously paid. The 'family fee' was abolished. Much more money was involved here. We had no choice really.

So finally after receiving my first immigration miracle 5 years later my family and I became permanent residents and within another 18 months, we were sworn in as citizens of the UK. Such a journey! But, thanks be to God, it all makes sense now.

Chapter Thirteen

My UK Miracles

*BORDERLINE CLINICAL DEPRESSION DIAGNOSED
*HEALING MIRACLE FROM DEPRESSION

*I*t all makes sense now!

Looking back too, I think my exposure to strong levels of stress, embarrassment and the uncertainty which loomed over our future in this country (as relates to leave to remain) might have contributed to my later diagnosis of 'borderline clinical depression'. This happened when Joshua was about 3 months old. It was a very difficult time for me trying to cope with all that was happening externally (pressures of being a mother third time round, job loss situation and this – Home Office discrepancies) as well as internally–the erratic operations of my hormones which left me in a very sad and tearful state for months.

On one of my early visits from my Health Visitor, she conducted a Health Questionnaire with me and found that my results suggested I needed to be seen by a General Practitioner (GP). She continued to explain to me that it was a bit concerning that although I had a very supportive husband and understanding lovely children, my scores are coming out so low. When I asked what she meant, her response shocked me. She told that I am coming up as being 'so sad' on too many occasions; hence her referral.

My visit to the GP's office revealed a shocking diagnosis for me. You see, I did not even realise that I was sad, as this Health Visitor had said; let alone to know that I was "so" sad. I did realise that I did not want to see people and that I was a bit withdrawn. But that was all I thought there was to it. However, the doctor did diagnose 'borderline clinical depression'. Needless to say, I was shocked at the diagnosis. I suddenly felt helpless. I felt I had now lost control of everything especially as I was not aware of what was happening to me.

I was indeed helpless at this point. So after hearing my diagnosis, I thought long and hard with all the strength that I could muster – as by now even thinking was more like a tedious chore for me – it was hard work for me to even engage my mind to think. Then I thought "I don't want this! I will not be depressed! No way!" Call it denial if you may. But I found some strength to think and know that 'depression' was not my portion. Therefore in my helpless state the only way I knew how to help myself was not to receive that diagnosis as my own. I knew that I had no intention of owning 'clinical depression' and it was never something I wish to own.

So with all the strength I had (because it was hard work to even think, then) I mustered the courage to say to my General Practitioner (GP) as he began to explain the meds I would need and as he reached for his prescription pad and pen:

"Please sir, do not write me that prescription."

He was clearly stunned at my statement. So he asked:

"Why, may I ask?" He enquired.

Then I replied to my dear Doctor S:

"Because, with due respect Sir, I will not be taking them; so please do not waste your time writing the prescription because I will not be taking them."

Doctor S looked at me as if I just landed from another planet or as if I had 'lost a screw' (a term used in Jamaica to mean 'coo-coo' or insane). He did look at me, hesitate and then finally he remarked to me:

"Well, Mrs Litchmore-Grant, if that's what you think, that is fine; but I know you will need these meds to allow you to sleep and the other (which he named only I cannot remember what that one was) to energize you during your waking hours."

Honestly, I did shock myself there in the doctor's office. IT DID NOT MAKE SENSE to me then. I had no idea where that boldness came from at that moment of my diagnosis; as I am not usually so assertive, at least not in my opinion. I did feel like someone was helping me then. As within myself I was indeed feeling very helpless at this time. I personally believe that my Comforter, the Holy Spirit, came to my rescue right there and then.

It all began to make sense as I was to be visited again by my Health Visitor 5 months later. During her second visit, she found that from the results of my second assessment questionnaire the ratings had greatly exceeded her expectations. She remarked: "Having had meds for 5 months, your results are way in excess of mine and the professional's expectations."

It was then that I was happy to inform her that I had not taken any medication at all. I thought I had busted her bubbles; but suddenly her face lit up with excitement. Then she asked me what had happened.

After explaining to my Health Visitor that I had not accepted the meds from my GP because I suddenly felt the urge to refuse it and not to accept 'clinical depression' as my own. She then asked me how I managed to have moved from such a low score to such high scores in just 5 short months without any medication. My response was simply "I prayed – I went down on my knees and prayed to God!"

She then smiled widely and said: "Now I can speak to you on another level, as a Christian myself." (She noted that they are not allowed to speak about their faith on the job but as I mentioned 'prayer' she needed to tell me something.) At this point she confided that when she left my home that day 5 months ago she became burdened with my results and my condition. She knew the GP would have needed to medicate me and so she instantly started praying for me. Little wonder I felt this unusual boldness at the point of the doctor's diagnosis in his office that day; hence my bold resistance to the medications being offered me (as previously mentioned). Someone somewhere was praying for me and surely the Holy Spirit came to my rescue.

It all makes sense now. Indeed!

During those five 'dark months' I was not aware of many things which people would take for granted on a daily basis. I struggled to understand why people were laughing or simply being happy, to make sense of places and roads which I normally knew, to understand my own feelings and identity (just indifferent), among other things.

People laughing and generally being happy would have irritated me so much. It was as if my mind was asking: "Who gave them the right to be so happy?" I could not make sense of this thought process, knowing the happy person I have always been. I have been a member of the Optimist Club International for some years while in Jamaica, working in the high school with young people. I used to be the one encouraging children and young adults to be happy and enjoy everything they do. My motto then was to 'look on the brighter side of life'. So this was a very strange place for me to have found myself in. It certainly did not make any sense to me whatsoever.

Making sense of places we would normally visit or simply identifying local roads we used time and time again was another of my struggles and frustrations, as I said before. Upon reflecting on the whole ordeal I thought this must have caused so much frustration to my dear husband, Linton, who had to be faced with the same nagging question over and over again: "Where are we now? Or "What road is this?" Later, when I was healed, I found out how frustrating this was for my family. They explained to me how I used to behave when we went on the road. That's when they succeeded in getting me to leave the house, in the first place. I still apologise to them years later.

The 'dark months' also saw me losing my personal identity. It was as if I did not remember who I was. It felt weird but again, I knew that I had no control over how I was feeling then. Nothing about me resembles anything I knew about myself all my life. I, being the decent well mannered, tidy and well-groomed young lady I had grown up to be, was changing. The most frustrating part of this 'dark period' was that I could perceive what was happening but I lost the ability to do anything about it. So, for instance, I would not want to have a shower–I did not feel the need to be clean and fresh.

As if that was not enough, I would wear one pair of trousers for 3-4 days and it was as if that was normal. I could see nothing wrong with that. Clearly my identity has changed to a different person. I had lost my identity. I would answer to my name but I had no idea who I was anymore. It was as if I was always surrounded by a dark cloud which was so thick and suffocating, I could not see my way. Believe me, it is very hard to explain.

I only found out about my loss of identity on the day I think 'the miracle' happened in our home in Marsh Farm, Luton. The penny dropped that day. Details of this day will follow shortly – Healing Miracle From Depression.

My greatest struggle, in retrospect, was the isolation which had gripped me. I would not be seen with anyone, not even my children. One day I remember shouting at my husband and children to get out of the house. The remarkable thing was that I could see and hear myself acting like this; I knew what I was doing was wrong BUT I had no power or will to correct it. This was very frustrating; not only for me but to my husband and children who were seeing the huge changes in my behaviour but felt helpless to effect any changes.

HEALING MIRACLE FROM DEPRESSION

My miracle took place after many prayers from family and friends. It is worth remarking here that during those 'dark moments' I could not even pray for myself. Yes, you read that correctly, a Christian from childhood, a pastor's wife for over 7 years (in Jamaica) and a Sunday school teacher, could not pray for herself. Only I did not know these things about myself during this time.

This is how I knew a miracle had taken place

One morning I decided to try tidying the bookshelves in the living room. I had strategized this 'huge cleaning project' because at that time in my life, any little job around the house turned out to be a 'big chore' for me. I just did not have the mental or physical strength to do anything, no matter how small. So I decided to clean one shelf that day; with the hope of cleaning another shelf the next day and so on.

As I got to the middle of the shelf a book happened to fall to the floor. Out of it fell 3 photographs. Slowly, I stooped to pick them up. When I saw the person on the photographs I struggled to determine who this young man was. I tried very hard to engage my mind to decipher who this person was. The first thing that stood out to me was the khahki uniform he was wearing. So

I thought of school uniform. But which school wear khahki? After a while the thought came – I suddenly remembered the Jamaican schools. The other thing I recognised from the photo was the he was posing with his head boy trophy and his school leaving certificate. Believe me, I really had to ponder these things in my mind for a few minutes well before arriving at an answer. I asked myself questions over and over – Who is this? Where is this?

The final thing that stood out from the third photo was that this young man was standing next to me presenting me with a gift basket. Then suddenly the penny dropped. I immediately heard myself saying "O my God! I was a teacher!" And instantly everything just looked brighter. Everything inside the house and when I looked outside, Wow! Everything seemed so bright. I began to see things I never saw before, although they were there all along. That was my miracle right there!

Then all on a sudden the dots were now connecting. This young man was a former head boy of the school where I worked in Jamaica for 12 years prior to migrating to the UK. He was a diligent and ambitious student who had just returned to Jamaica after completing a bachelor degree in USA. According to him, he had 'returned to work with me in the ICT department as a thank you for believing in him and supporting him to get this scholarship which took him to the USA.'

The student and his mum had come to visit me at my home in Greater Portmore on the weekend before my family and I left Jamaica for the United Kingdom. These three photos were part of his gift, along with a delicious cake, he and his Mum brought me to remember them when I leave. Wow! If ever these photos were meant to be blessing to me, they were definitely my blessing that day. This was my miracle there – I finally remembered who I was. Those three photos did it! IT ALL MAKES SENSE NOW!

Chapter Fourteen

The 'Shut-Up Syndrome' In Church

*TESTS TO BUILD MY FAITH
*ABBI'S SCARY DREAM
*THE 'SHUT-UP SYNDROME' IN BUSINESS
*MOST EMBARASSING MOMENT
*TIME TO MOVE ON
*HOW HAVE THINGS CHANGED

THE 'SHUT-UP SYNDROME' IN CHURCH

Not very long after arriving in the UK many cultural biases were evident in various circles. These included the secular work environment, the business environment and my church environment. In my opinion these biases seemed to have been more entrenched in my church circles. Other church denominations we visited seemed quite welcoming and embracing. One example of these cultural biases is what I call the 'shut-up syndrome'.

The 'shut-up syndrome' is a term an elderly friend, Miss Ruby (not her real name), introduced to me some time ago. It is what she referred to as constant deliberate efforts to suppress and prevent another person from speaking or expressing their thoughts. This could even be extended to mean deliberately withholding a platform from an individual. From our experiences, my husband and I concluded this syndrome as conscious efforts to shut us up. These were especially evident after receiving positive feedbacks from our various audiences. The shock about this was that at first our preaching and teaching were generally well accepted by the perpetrators. Initially there was no problem at all. Then suddenly it appeared as if all hell broke loose. How sad!

From my observation over the years, and after some enlightening conversations with my elderly friend Miss Ruby, I have concluded, based on her insights, that this 'shut-up syndrome' as she puts it, has its inception in the personality traits of most of our leaders. She believed that perpetrators of this 'shut-up syndrome' operated from a place of insecurity and low self-esteem; especially among those who were born around 1950's-1960's. Miss Ruby, who has children born in this country as well as some who were born in Jamaica, saw first-hand the differences the cultures make in their personalities and their outlook at life. She advised that a lot of these people do not like foreigners who are intelligent and educated. They will try to keep you down. Therefore she warned me to look out for such behavioural traits and encouraged me to be strong.

Her conclusion was based on a seemingly unofficial 'social research' conducted via observation of her own two sets of children and those of numerous families with Caribbean parentage (mostly her associates). Her philosophy was that after their arrival in the UK during the 50s and 60s pregnant Caribbean mothers were forced to suppress their identities and their true qualities – herself included. As a result she felt the children born then tended to have identity problems and suffered from low self-esteem issues. Food for thought indeed! Coming from a layman or a laywoman, in this case.

Although I was fore-warned, when some incidents occurred they still had me baffled for a while. It just did not seem to make any sense to me. Then various questions started flying around in my mind: 'Who stands to gain from such callus behaviours? Where is the people's spiritual conviction anyway? Who are they serving, really?'

It is my belief that if God is living on the inside of an individual then they should be no need to feel insecure or intimidated by anyone, despite their educational background, personal achievements or anything at all. God is no respector of persons anyway. After all God expects us to love one another and in doing so, we will be kind one to another. 1 John 4:20 "Whoever claims to love God yet hates his brother or sister is a liar. For whoever does not love their brother and sister, whom they have seen, cannot love God, whom they have not seen." (NIV)

Thankfully after some years' experience and a master's degree in psychology later, I am now better able to put the pieces of the puzzle together. I started to make sense of such behaviours. I was motivated to study psychology to make sense of human's thinking and behaviours in order to help myself and to be of help on a wider scale than just in the classroom. What I did not know then, was that the churches I attended would be my first testing ground. It certainly does make sense NOW!

Although it is hard to speak about such negative cultural traits, hopefully this 'shut-up syndrome' would shed some light into unexplainable incidents, should there be others out there who are facing similar situations. It is my hope that sharing these 'shut-up syndrome' experiences will be a source of empowerment. The word of James has been my source of strength during those trying times. 'Knowing this, that the trying of your faith worketh patience. But let patience have her perfect work, that ye may be perfect and entire." (James 3:3-4). It is therefore, my hope that highlighting these experiences will help to identify and eliminate some cultural barriers within the church and the wider society. Often the victims are likely to be left scarred and wounded unless they experience supernatural healing power.

In order to give a first-hand understanding of these cultural biases I will start with my personal experience. I hasten to report that during the process of understanding these cultural biases confessions, apologies, forgiveness and restoration have occurred among all parties involved. Thankfully we are all at a better place now with great friendships.

I can remember at least three occasions in which I have been asked to prepare to preach in church. To my utter surprise and disgust, on the appointed day I was not even called upon. Yes, you read that correctly! I was not called upon at all. In fact on one of those occasions, I observed someone else being introduced as the preacher. Sadly, this behaviour was often followed with neither an explanation nor an apology. I felt this was different. I wondered, did they forgot that they had asked me to prepare to speak?

I did wonder to myself: "Why am I allowing myself to be treated with such disdain over and over again?" You might be wondering the same thing as well. But by nature I am not a confrontational person. This happens to be a trait that both my husband, Linton, and I possess. After all, coming from a warm and friendly Jamaican culture, we tend to be laid back by nature. Let alone being pushy or confrontational.

In fact the similar fate was also meted out to my husband, prior to my own experience. He did allow himself to go through that experience three times before he finally did something about it. Patient man! The fact is that this 'shut-up syndrome' actually started with him – 'the Pastor from Jamaica' as he was called. Upon realising what was going on, I advised him to speak to the leaders about it before it continued and extended to me as well. Well, you may have guessed it. He did nothing about it until after about the third occasion. Inevitably the 'shut-up syndrome' continued until it spilled over to me. Long, long sufferers, indeed! Or were we just foolish? I choose to believe that we were simply 'long sufferers'.

The culture shock accompanied with migrating to this 'cold' country, lasted much longer than I had expected. The coldness in the weather was more bearable than the coldness in attitudes we often faced. Although we've had some great positive experiences shortly after our arrival, we were met with many situations which we found to be very challenging and often stiflingly difficult to cope with – a real culture shock! We just could not make sense of lots of these behaviours. To be clear the word 'we' refers to my husband, my eldest daughter and I (our youngest daughter was too young to understand what was happening). Remarkably we did find a common thread running through a set of people belonging to a specific age group, born to a specific group of Caribbean islanders. This is what my elderly friend, Miss Ruby had referred to as 'shut-up syndrome' which existed inside and outside my church circles.

Often in this 'shut-up syndrome' I would find myself asking the obvious questions: "Did they forget they had asked me to share a testimony or a message?" "Why did they bother to ask me in the first place? Do they not know it takes time and effort to prepare for this?" Sadly, very often the responses were without any apology. I felt something had to be wrong. Very wrong. This was so frustrating. It just did not make any sense.

Given that we were strangers in this country, we considered the church members as our new family. There were some dramatic changes and some valid lessons learned. However we found solace in the words of Paul to the Ephesians church when he says: "For we do not wrestle against flesh and blood, but against principalities, against powers, against the rulers of the darkness of this age, against spiritual *hosts* of wickedness in the heavenly *places." (Ephesians 6:12 NKJV)*

Given the repetitive nature of this 'shut-up syndrome' I was still unable to make full sense of what was happening then. Additionally, another sad fact was that this was still happening even after ten years. Once again I was left so burdened with not being given the chance to share, even though I have been asked to and had prepared to share. The cultural difference here was startling, as back home you would always encouraged to share your testimony; and if for any reason you were not called upon as planned, it would be explained to you right away and an apology given, as warranted. Not an issue at all!

Worthy of note too is the fact that this 'shut up syndrome' was not unique to my church circles. I recall the identical response being given me after I had been asked to share my business testimony in a business conference, a few years later. Not surprising–the audience is of a similar background to my church. These are two different platforms but such similar experiences.

Now that I am in church leadership here in the UK and since I have made some sense of this 'shut-up syndrome,' I endeavour to look for opportunities to give people a chance to develop and grow, much the same way that I am used to operating anyway as a teacher and mentor.

'SHUT UP SYNDROME' IN BUSINESS

Then there were the occasions of this 'shut-up syndrome' even among my business associates here in the UK. Like I said before, it is not unique to our church culture. At this point I literally began to believe the lie of the enemy that 'something must be wrong with me'. Could it be my accent, my voice, my demeanour, my content, my dress? Of course nothing was obviously wrong with any of those scenarios cited, but the questions kept coming to my head. What could it be then? Sadly I always seemed to think it had to do with me. Only later to find out it had nothing to do with me.

It was so confusing for me. To put it mildly, I felt rejected and isolated. Especially as I am an immigrant with all our friends and relatives back home, these make for very lonely times. To discover that it was among the people we knew here and taken as our new family that we experienced this 'shut us up syndrome'. It was clearly a pattern. There was nothing I could do about the culture but tried to deal with it as best as possible. Well, I did go into a depressive silence for a while.

It was easy to give up and say: 'That's it. I've had enough." At one point I even decided to keep myself to myself. I thought "If I stay 'shut-up' then I will not be put in a position to be embarrassed or rejected." That of course was the easy alternative. It cost me my business in the end. When I think back to what God has done for me, I am even more excited now to share about His love and His grace with other people. Hopefully, I am doing that now via this medium.

This shut-up syndrome was a season in my life from which I have learned many life lessons in and out of the church. Then I finally realised that all along it was never about me, but it was about the call of God on my life. It is worth mentioning at this time that seasons, by their very nature, do not last. This too will pass.

TESTS TO BUILD MY FAITH

Why would I want to testify anyway? For me whenever I go through a test or series of trials I found spending time in prayer and the Word give me more strength. I have also learned to ask others to pray with me. I recall a particular group of believers prayed for me collectively, after I was allowed to share my testimony. To God be the glory! I did get a breakthrough and felt the heaviness of bereavement and spiritual oppression lifted that day. Praise God for the praying believers.

These feelings of heaviness and oppression did come after a series of events which left members our family worn down and depressed. We had lost five close relatives in five short months in 2012. Therefore having had a breakthrough, I was motivated to share this with the people who had collectively prayed for me a few months prior. However, I was not allowed. Not enough time. I got it now!

Immediately following that specific experience – another dimension of what I call 'shut up' experience, I sat pondering about it and started feeling sorry for myself. Suddenly I heard Holy Spirit said to me some reassuring words: "Don't worry my child! One day you will have your own platform to speak the mind of the Father to many people. I am proud of you and I will be proud of you, my daughter!"

Wow! I felt so relieved. I felt comforted by those words; they gave me hope. That was a glorious moment for me.

Prior to and since then I have had many trials but most importantly, I have also had many miracles which ultimately brought me and my family many break-throughs. Praise God! I will explore some of these trials through which God brought us out victoriously. Among the challenges were things like having to make several trips to the hospital A&E with the children with unexplained illnesses. These included – One morning our first daughter woke up unable to walk and had to be rushed to hospital. Doctors, despite consulting their medical book, still could not make a diagnosis of her condition. This caused our faith to be put in action. For sure these trials, possibly designed to break me, did make my faith stronger in the end.

So while one child was unwell with an undiagnosed situation, our second daughter, Abbi got ill later that same week. It followed shortly by her waking up with terrible stomach pains and exceptionally high temperature, which rendered her unable to walk upright. I was becoming overwhelmed at this point, with a baby to look after as well.

A few years later there were other distractions. The unexplained heart palpitations and chest pains – two of our three children in a matter of two weeks had to be rushed to A&E by ambulance. Then there were freak accidents–sprains, fractures, knee dislocations (our first daughter had two dislocations in as many weeks).

Things continued to go crazy around us for a while but in every instance God provided divine protection. One Sunday morning while helping my husband remove some fried dumplings from the fryer, the boiling hot oil exploded on my face, arm and chest. (Remember I am a born Jamaican and Jamaicans love their fried dumplings). This was to be followed not long afterwards by two minor motor vehicle accidents in which I suffered whiplashes. Then my son, Joshua, suffered minor head injuries in a minor bus accident.

Then there were some social distractions as well. These involved the egging of our home and our car graffitied. On at least two occasions we woke up to find our windows egged. Then another day as I went to get in my car for work, I recognised it had been sprayed with a black paint across its entire length. It was a red car graffitied in black. We were told that the word sprayed on it was also socially unacceptable. Wow!

Considering that these events among others, all happened within a few years; it was becoming overwhelming. But thankfully I looked back with a sense of gratitude because in all these incidents we suffered no long term damage. Thank you Lord! I praise you in the good times and in the bad!

ABBI'S SCARY DREAM

Abbi's stomach ache, mentioned above, was preceded by a dream she had during the night. She dreamt that a church leader had forced her to have a meal containing eye balls, tongues, ears and other body parts. In the dream she refused the meal because she did not want to eat 'those things' according to her. But at the coaxing of her Dad, who did not want to upset the church leader, she reluctantly tried the food. She said as a result she felt sick in the dream.

It is my firm belief that this dream resulted in her physically eliminating this 'freaky meal' from her system onto the bed that night. A real terrible experience for my five year old daughter and for myself, who had to clean up. That night, unaware of her dream then, as I returned to my bedroom the Holy Spirit prompted me to go back to their room to pray over the girls. Only to wake up the next morning to see a physically sick child. Again, there were no proper diagnosis from the medical practitioners – just speculations.

Having journaled some of the various situations my family and I were facing on a consistent basis, I felt we had no breathing space at all. It was so overwhelming, I did find writing them down to be therapeutic for me. I described these experiences as 'spiritual oppressive situations'. They did seem to me that a lot was happening– one thing after the other. I felt these things were very oppressive but to God be the glory for His mighty works in our lives! Thankfully we were protected from anything life threatening or permanent. Praise God! Praise God!

Most Embarrassing Moment

This meeting actually happened following one of the most embarrassing experiences I had in church and remember, I have been a member of the church for over 30 years at that time. I refer to the next event as my 'most embarrassing moment'. I am happy to report that reconciliation between all parties involved in this scenario of my life have been achieved. A better friendship developed as a result. We are all at a better place today because of the understanding we all gained as a result of this experience. Certainly it all make sense now!

The 'most embarrassing moment' for me may have been a 'look over' for many, but with my self-esteem being shaky by that time, it was hard for me then. Unfortunately it seemed I had started to believe the lie of the enemy as to my own personality. One day I was asked by a director to bring the message at the next monthly ministry service. Two weeks before the date I received a call from her informing me that the pastor had asked someone else to be a guest speaker on that day, possibly a case of miscommunication. She apologised. So I thanked her for letting me know.

However, a few days before the date, I received another call. This time she explained that the invited 'guest speaker' will not be able to make it so if I would be willing to go ahead and prepare to speak on the Sunday. Reluctantly, I accepted. Honestly, I did feel a sense of uneasiness about the whole thing. But because I had agreed, I decided to do my best by the help of God.

To my surprise, and by now I should not be surprised anymore, but…yes, you guessed it! I was not even called upon. In fact that day I happened to have got somewhat of an apology from the pastor who led the service from start to finish. Again the question resurfaced. Why would they ask me to prepare to preach and yet again did not call on me? It was embarrassing indeed.

Fortunately for me, as things turned out that day, I was not alone in church to witness this 'embarrassing moment'. My hairdresser while working on my hair the day before (Saturday), she felt the unction of the Holy Spirit so strongly that she started speaking in tongues over my head. Wow! That was strange. Given I was getting a hairdo and then this. This was a real case of 'God moving in mysterious ways.'

She literally had to stop working as she began prophesying over me and my husband who was on vacation in Jamaica at the time (and whom she had never met). Her prophecy was a direct confirmation to one we had been given a few years earlier by Minister Tony Miller – shortly after we arrived in the UK. Then she announced to me: "Sorry Jane, but I must be with you in your church tomorrow." She said that she was compelled by the Holy Spirit to do so. However, her obedience to the voice of God came with a personal sacrifice on her part. She had to put off attending her God-daughter's christening that same morning.

Not only was my hairdresser there to witness the treatment I received in the place of worship; there happened to be some other strangers who witnessed it as well – totally unplanned. Linton's friend and his wife were visiting us that same weekend. They decided to accompany me to church that morning, so they too saw this treatment first-hand. If it had not happened to me, I would not have believed something like this could happen in the body of Christ. But thankfully there were witnesses (visitors) who are born again and possess the spirit of discernment. At the end of the service my hair dresser sternly asked me: "What are you doing in a place like this?" Strong words to ponder.

When I got home that day I cried like a baby. I laid prostrate before the Lord with one question. On my belly in the living room, I cried out to the Lord for the answer. "Why, Lord...Why?"

Not long after that event my husband and I met up with the leader to make sense of the events of that day which was clearly embarrassing for me. But unfortunately instead of getting an answer as to why, the blame was seemingly laid at my feet. In essence I was seemingly being accused of not 'knowing how to flow with the spirit'. So I needed to learn to flow in the spirit. No real apology was given except to say that no embarrassment was intended. Maybe I needed to learn something new about operations in church. I don't know.

Fortunately or unfortunately, this meeting triggered my motivation to leave – I had had enough. The response I received was quick and direct. "That's OK. If you want to leave you leave. I can't stop people who say they want to leave." Reference was also made of the couple who left the previous year exactly. There were no apologies, no questions asked as to how I was really feeling and what if anything could be done to help appease the situation, especially given that I was serving in the church. Can you imagine how I felt the following Sunday when I heard words to this effect from the podium: "If people want to leave, they can leave. I will miss you but go if you want to go, go." At this point I was still learning about church culture and church operations in the UK.

Knowing that I had made my intention known (leaving) in our recent meeting, I felt like I was punched in the stomach when I heard it. I could not believe what I was hearing. It was crippling! But one thing was sure, a decision needed to be made soon. There was no reason for me to allow myself to be abused in such a subtle and evil way any longer. My grandmother used to say: 'God called fools but he does not keep them.' In essence He makes them wise.

Amazingly, the Lord helped me to overcome this ordeal in a very short time. It's a miracle how He helped me to quickly forgive everyone involved. THE POWER OF FORGIVENESS! This was a big change in me who normally would find it difficult to let go of things. That was how I knew I had grown from this experience. Thank God, He has turned what was meant for bad into my good! You see, I had several intercessors who were filling heaven with prayers on our behalves. From that crippling experience I realised I had two choices – to be bitter or better. Thankfully I chose to be 'better' for it. I decided to quickly forgive and that works–after much crying, praying and receiving many prophetic words. Once again it became clear that it was time for us to move on. Praise God! In retrospect, IT ALL MAKES SENSE NOW!

Let me hasten to say that as the Lord would have it, the same visiting church where I experienced my 'most embarrassing moment' happens to be our first pastoral appointment in the UK only a few years later. Coincidence? I do not think so. There are none of those with God. He does not do coincidence.

Just over a year after our appointment I happened to deliver the same message that I was prevented from delivering on that fateful 'embarrassing' day. It was entitled 'To Know Christ and to Make Him Known'. My mess seems to have become my message after all. God is truly amazing! IT ALL MAKES SENSE NOW!

TIME TO MOVE ON

We have had several incidents pointing to this time to move on. Our final decision came after my husband and I were informed that we were 'no longer needed in the leadership team' of the church. Exactly one hour before the leadership meeting was due to start, we received a phone call in which we were informed that my husband's service was no longer required on the leadership team. The leader went on to also inform him that he no longer will be appointing me (the wife) to the position he had previously spoken to me about.

When my husband asked for a reason such sudden decision was made, he was told that it was just a 'gut feeling'. So my husband asked whether it had anything to do with something he or I had said or done. Again the response was 'No. It's just gut instinct'. At this point I remembered my husband asking him about the role of the Holy Spirit in such decision to which he was told that it was not a directive from the Holy Spirit. Linton thanked him for the call. Understandably we were both stunned. But accepted our fate.

At the meeting that night, the leaders were told that we were no longer required on the leadership team where my husband had been 'co-ordinator'. There was visible shock on all the faces. There were questions coming from left, right and centre. Most members seemed confused. All questions were seemingly answered with the same words: 'They have done me nothing. But it is my gut feelings'. At that point we felt quite uncomfortable. Then my husband spoke out finally:

"With due respect, If you can't say what we have done or said to offend you, then you have put us in an awkward position. As we might continue to do and say things which may offend you in the future and we would not have known it. So I don't think we can continue working with you under such conditions." We then notify the leaders of our decision.

One month later we left in a 'less than desirable way'. Exactly one year after another family had left. Our children were badly affected by the move despite the four weeks' notice we had to prepare them. Each of our children was given a card with a crying child and the words 'We will miss you' written on it. It seemed strange! Even on the day of our leaving proved no different. The fact was that the brethren were only told of our leaving on the day we were leaving. "Awkward!"

How queer? But that was what it was. One lady in particular would have liked to do something worthwhile for us but her hands were figuratively tied. Unfortunately or fortunately, on the day of our departure there were some visitors from another of our area churches. They bore witness of this 'send off'. One actually remarked afterwards 'If someone had told me how this 'send off' of a minister and his family was done I would not have believed it.' Then I realised that we were not alone in believing something must be wrong here. It probably was not general church culture after all.

So much for a 'send off!' We were all to learn from the experience. In my opinion this kind of behaviour had rejection and dejection written all over it. Our young children were quite upset at the time but thankfully, they soon found fellowship with another congregation. With good advice and teachings on forgiveness we were able to deal with this unpleasant experience. It was hard but we were determined not to stay and wallow in self-pity.

As a family we realised we were on a real spiritual journey. We spent some time worshipping in the comfort of our home until we felt led to a specific congregation. Here we had time to heal and felt the warmth of loving fellowship. A couple of years later, we happened to get a call from our regional bishop which was to change the trajectory of our spiritual journey.

The bishop spoke to us about him prayerfully seeking the Lord for a church leader and thought to approach us about it. He wanted to ascertain our opinion on the matter. Having walked with us through our earlier 'not so pleasant' church experience, he felt that our leadership qualities could be an asset.

As leadership was never something we aspired to or even thought about, we needed some time to process it. After all this was a shock to us. Therefore we asked for time to pray and process what taking up that appointment would mean to us as a family. We needed to think through the impact it would have on our work and children. It was a scary prospect but we were prepared to pray and wait on the Lord for His directives.

Within a few days of us praying about our decision we had two weird experiences. These were in the form of telephone harassment. One night, well early morning, we got a phone call that awoke us from our deep sleep. The person on the other line had an Asian accent. He hurled abusive words at us jeering our Christianity. This was followed by a string of expletives. Then on day seven, we were awakened from our sleep in the early hours of the morning by another phone call. The caller said he was from the police department in our area. After he gave his name and ID number, he proceeded to inform us that it had been brought to his attention that we were using or harbouring users of cannabis in our home. The alleged police proceeded to warn that they would be coming to our house to conduct a search. He continued to threaten that if on their arrival we did not open the door then he would be breaking it down in order to do his search.

We thought the telephone calls were distractions orchestrated from the pit of hell. These events caused us to think long and hard about our pending decision. Then we realised that we needed to do something about it. We were convinced that regardless of the enemy's tricks he was already defeated through the blood and power of Jesus Christ our Lord. The next morning we made the call to the Bishop.

Soon afterwards our pastor was told of our pending appointment. He was pleased for us and he then prepared the congregation for our move. They all gave us their blessings, love and support. Our children too had to be prepared for this move. They were even negotiating their willingness to share their time between the two churches. But unfortunately for them, that would have been difficult. Therefore, after a lovely send-off we were released to take up service in another town.

To God be the glory! We were inaugurated there on Easter Sunday 2010. We could not desire a better acceptance and welcome. The life lesson I learnt here was that the difficult times and tests were worth it. Having pastored two congregations in Jamaica prior, we never knew what to expect in this new environment. It was a daunting prospect. But we prayed and we had the prayerful support of our spiritual mentors (the National overseer of Jamaica and the Cayman Islands and our senior pastor Bishop Wilson), family and friends. Most of all, as His servants, we wanted to be obedient to God's calling on our lives.

As life throws challenges at us, even in leadership, we are able to use our experiences to strengthen our walk with God as well as to help others. I reflect on David who although he was anointed king did not sit on a throne until many years later. During that time he suffered rejection, ridicule, isolation, loneliness and hatred even among his own but he never gave up. After all, he was chosen and anointed. It all makes sense now!

HOW HAVE THINGS CHANGED?

It is all making sense now! Seasons change indeed. Following a 'shut up syndrome' season I now see the word of the Lord coming to pass so prominently in my life–just as He said to me at the conference a few years ago. The prophecies I have received in the past have begun to come to pass. Now, to my surprise, I am being invited by people (some of whom I do not even know personally), to be the guest speaker for various occasions, not only here in the UK but also abroad. These included being the guest speaker for a Graduation and Carol Service at my former place at work in Jamaica. Unfortunately, I could not attend the graduation but I did travel to the Carol Service (2008).

Then here in the UK, I have been invited to be guest speaker at World Day of Prayer 2013 event (while as vice-chair to Churches Together in Hitchin). It was no coincidence that the topic I was asked to address was 'I was a Stranger and You Welcomed Me.' Then I was asked to preach the Chairman's Sermon at my inauguration as Churches Together in Hitchin chair (January 2014). Also I was invited to be a guest speaker (one of a panel of five) at the recently held Go For Growth

Conference in Welwyn Garden City, Hertfordshire (3rd Oct 2015). This conference was facilitated by the Rev Dr Callan Slipper, director of Churches Together in Hertfordshire.

My recent invitations came only a couple of weeks ago (January 2016) at both regional and national levels. The truth is I am still baffled that I was the one they chose to invite. I thought to myself "Why me?" I didn't even know how these invitees heard about me, as I am someone that hardly knows anyone in authority. In retrospect however, the 'shut-up syndrome' I had experienced over the years is now becoming more understandable to me. This was certainly a season I had to go through. God clearly had a plan for my life. I recall His comforting voice resounding in my ears some time ago when He said to me: 'Don't worry my child. You will have your platform one day. I am proud of you!' It all makes sense now!

Jeremiah 29:11 states: "For I know the plans I have for you," declares the LORD, "plans to prosper you and not to harm you, plans to give you hope and a future" (NIV).

Chapter Fifteen

I Saw The Lord!

A. I SAW THE LORD!
B. GOD REVEALED THE SHIFT IN THE ATMOSPHERE
C. PROPHECIES
D. WIFE OF A PASTOR

I SAW THE LORD!

On Sunday 15th December 2013 I had an encounter with the Lord in a dream. A remarkable experience. That was a dream I did not wish to be awaken from. On that day our family was due to be going to a special service of thanksgiving for our five relatives who died in 2012 (5 in as many months). In the dream I saw myself being bitten on my right arm by a black bug. Suddenly I noticed something about the bug. Its back was shiny but upon closer inspection it was rough and gruffly. As I shook off the bug it mutated into two and this time both flew on me. Before they could bite me I quickly shook off those two bugs as well, and again they mutated into four. Then the four came back and I shook them off as well then the four became eight.

It continued like this until I was surrounded by a swarm of black bugs determined to kill me. Realising my fate I looked up towards the sky and said Lord, don't tell me these bugs are going to kill me out here. And immediately I saw the heavens opened and a huge beam of light in the form of a huge man stepping out and coming towards me. His countenance shone so brightly. As He came towards me the bugs all made a 'bee line' and hastily retreated from the light of His presence.

The Lord then came over to me. He wrapped His loving arms around me. Instantly, I became aware of the arms of the Lord covering and cuddling me. He was so tall, my face literally rested on the lower part of His chest. I could even feel His heartbeats. I felt such love and protection, I can't explain it. Then, suddenly, I found myself standing a couple metres away looking on myself being cuddled by the Lord. At that moment I heard myself saying, 'O, that is my Lord and He has come to rescue me from these deadly bugs.' Then once again I found myself wrapped in His huge arms and felt the warmth of His embrace. As I was becoming comfortable I woke out of the dream.

Wow! It's the first time I felt disappointed to wake out of a dream. Who could blame me? It was such a wonderful place of love, warmth, protection and comfort, I just didn't want the experience to end. That dream was to be my saving grace which protected and comforted me in the ensuing years of trials and betrayal. Thank you Lord, You came and rescued me! It all make sense now.

God Revealed a Shift in the Atmosphere

One thing that still puzzles me is the mighty way God revealed His spiritual shift to me and my family recently. After all He is God, and He is unfathomable. We have heard the word of the Lord through various prophetic voices that God is bringing about a 'shift in the atmosphere'. Only we had no idea how God was going to do this shifting. It was amazing yet painful to say the least. As the scenario is still fresh in my psyche I will spare the unpleasant details.

The sense of betrayal and loss of people we held dear were not what we had envisioned the shifting would mean. But when things unfolded we had to accept them. God did some shifting and we are trusting God for His continued grace and mercy. Thank you Lord! It all makes sense now!

The remarkable thing is that since my inauguration as chairman of Churches Together in Hitchin in 2014 we have seen a shift in our local congregation. The secretary of CTH, John Richardson did inform me that my appointment was historic on two levels. It was the first time since its 50 years inception that a black person was appointed as chairman to CTH and secondly, it was the first time that a Pentecostal was to hold the position. Members of the 18-members churches council were delighted to have me on board along with all the other members of our church. Yes, I travelled over 6,000 miles to live here in the UK because God had a plan. This was probably yet another shift in the atmosphere orchestrated by the heavenly Father. Praise God, it is all making sense to me now.

PROPHECIES

During my Christian journey I have had several prophetic word spoken over me. Some have come to pass and others are yet to be fulfilled. Not to be naive, some were false. No coincidence here! Scripture tells us in 1 John 4:1 'Beloved believe not every spirit, but try the spirits and whether they are of God: because many false prophets are gone out into the world. (NIV)

One of the first true prophetic word I received was from my local church pastor, Steadman Haase. He took my left hand and raised the ring finger and said that one day this finger will be given over to a minister. At the time I started to think 'ok, we'll see'. I was sceptical. But nine years later it came to pass. It was during our engagement that I remembered the prophecy. When I informed my pastor of the engagement he asked whether my fiancée was a minister. Then I realised that pastor's prophecy was about to come to pass. After being engaged for a year my husband-to-be was appointed to the ministry. What could I do? Even though I wanted to stay far away from the ministry because of what I had observed so far, I refused to stand in his way.

In those days, my husband and other newly appointed pastors were only told of their appointments during the National Convention – no previous warning or notification was given. Thank God this system has changed now! So you can imagine the shock I had then when I received the call from Linton to say that he is being appointed as pastor of the church in Font Hill, St Thomas. Yes you guessed it, he was calling from the National Convention in 1995. Since we are already engaged there was no turning back for me. Then I realised that with Linton's appointment the prophecy was about to come to pass. To God be the glory!

Another prophecy I recall with honour to God was given in Connecticut, USA. Linton had been invited to preach at the church where his brother served as an associate pastor. During the service one of the pastors came to where I was sitting and called me out. She prophesied about my decision to resign my job and gave me a directive to go back and love, honour and not be resentful of my boss. The truth is, I still had my resignation letter in my handbag when she told me those things. I had made up my mind that on my return from vacation I would hand in my resignation from the job due to the seven years struggles I have had there. But, God changed my plan.

As this woman of God continued her prophecy, I found that God must have planned for me, although I was far from home. Additionally, she told me that the doctors may have said I cannot have children but God wants me to know that He is opening my womb and I shall bear not just a child but children, who will be dedicated to Him. Right away I knew that this total stranger who knew nothing about me could only be hearing from the Lord. She did hit the nail on its head. Thanks be to God that prophecy has come through in such a remarkable way. (See Our Baby Miracle). We now have three beautiful children who love and serve the Lord Jesus Christ.

Since we migrated to the UK I have received at least three prophecies which have come to pass. I recall one such prophecy from Pastor Tony Miller. His words were regarding my call to speak in different nations. In less than a month this prophecy was fulfilled. I was called to be a guest speaker at my previous school in Jamaica. When I asked what led to their decision to have me to come from so far to speak to them there, what I was told warmed my heart. For that I give all the praise and honour to my God.

I was told that since I left the school it seemed that the presence of God was lifted. I asked the lady who gave me the invitation what she meant and she explained that since I have left the vice principal had died, another senior member of staff committed suicide and that gang violence had recently erupted on the school compound. This gang violence resulted in one young man's hand being almost severed. She also informed me that sadly, the staff prayer meeting I had started in the school had been discontinued a couple years after I migrated.

So sometimes you may get a prophetic word and you may think 'will it ever happen to me?' Yes, in a matter of time God will let His word come to pass in your life. Isaiah 55:11 states:

'So shall My word be that goes forth from My mouth; It shall not return to Me void, but it shall accomplish what I please, and it shall prosper *in the thing* for which I sent it.' (NKJV)

Even if it is something you may not desire, God knows what is best for you. I can say this today because that was my thinking before. But now, It all makes sense now!

The Wife of a pastor.

Often as life throws up challenges we look back on some positive experiences of the past to cushion our pain and to give us hope to carry on. Once we learnt that Linton was first appointed as pastor in 1995, we committed our journey to the Lord. Not knowing what to expect, we embraced the call in obedience. We were blessed to be chosen to serve a small congregation over fifty miles from our home. Having to take three or sometimes four different transports to get there. This small farming community was to be transformed by the power of God in the five years we spent there. When we were leaving Font Hill we left a finished building, a great improvement on the building frame we saw when we first arrived.

Not only was the infrastructure improved, but most importantly, the lives of the members were greatly improved as well – spiritually and physically. Using his influence as an employee of the National Training Agency in Jamaica my husband helped several young people to educate themselves. My role was just an encourager but they are grateful for it, as they speak about it every time they happen to speak about us. Today several young Jamaicans have become professionals and are making valuable contributions to the society and to the church, specifically. Our then church clerk, Cynthia, is now a senior pastor in the area with responsibilities as area supervisor. To God be all the glory!

Needless to say that the love and respect shown to us by these people was phenomenal. So too was our second pastorate, in Naggo's Head, Portmore. The opportunity God had given us to work with another congregation for two years prior to us leaving Jamaica had concretised our faith in what God can do if you remain faithful. We are thankful for the able leadership of Bishop Novel Wilson with whom we are still in contact. There were many experiences which today still bring a smile to my face and joy to my heart, especially when we face the rejection and other negative experiences here in the UK.

Thanks be to God for the seeds we have sown in those lives and for the seeds we are still sowing in many lives today by God's grace, even though we go through some tough times. I give thanks to God Almighty for the people in the church here in the UK who continue to be a blessing to us; and they are many. There are clearly more that are with us than those that are against us. Their prayers and support help to keep us grounded especially when the going gets tough. As I reminisce, It all makes sense now!

Chapter Sixteen

My Time As Chairman Of Churches Together In Hitchin (Cth)

O ne of the great highlights working alongside my husband as a newly appointed pastor was that we hosted a 50th Year celebration of the church in the town of Hitchin. The very next day after a magnificent Jubilee celebration I was greeted with the devastating news that my uncle in New York had died. He was the uncle who my family should have been visiting that summer for a reunion. Now he was gone. As he was the fifth relative of both our families to die in that year, well within five months, I felt my world came crashing down. To add to this loss three days later I found our pet rabbit Lucy dead in her cage. You can imagine the sadness and grief we suffered. Thankfully I was open to get help and after some months of bereavement counselling my children and I were doing much better. Unknown to me God had a plan. There was more for me to do in the town.

After an up and down year in 2012 the next year started with some remarkable happenings for me which I believe were God appointed. The New Year began with me finding a job and securing a good contract. I was now able to help my husband to provide for the family. I felt God was in this. But what happened next still baffles me. Later that year I received a call from Minister John Richardson, the secretary of Churches Together in Hitchin which shocked me beyond my wildest dreams. He informed me of the executive's decision to appoint me as vice chair to CTH for 2013 if I would say 'yes'. He explained that this would lead to me taking on the full chairmanship in 2014. In the shock I heard myself asked him a string of questions without pausing to hear any response. 'Me? Why me? Vice-chair, what is that? What exactly am I expected to do?'

After John spoke a bit about how the CTH executive came to the decision of asking me to take on this position I managed to compose myself. Then I was able to hear his responses to the many questions I had pelted at him. He was so kind to go through them with me. He informed me that after a presentation I had made at my first council meeting a few months earlier, they spotted talents in me. This inspired some of the executive members to enquire and subsequently sought to find out more about me. It was then that I remembered that the then chairman, Trish, had requested a meeting with me and my family as my husband was a newly appointed pastor in the area. During that meeting nothing, and I mean absolutely nothing, was said about any intention of inviting me to the executive board of CTH.

Looking back now I thought that might have been a case of 'playing it safe' maybe. But I do see the logics here. Because it is always good to get background knowledge of those who are new among us, especially those being considered for leadership roles. That, I believe is wisdom.

John continued to explain another reason for their selection was the fact that the executive body had never had a Pentecostal being chairman and a member of the ethnic group, in this case a black person. He informed me that I was making history on two fronts. Suddenly I was faced with an opportunity of a lifetime. I decided to embrace the opportunity. I then made a promise to John that if he promised to guide me into this role then I am willing to give it a go. He promised he would, especially in his role as secretary. Then I accepted. I heard myself saying to him 'I will. I will do it if you promise to pray for me and tell me what I need to do.' This was a leap of faith on my part, trusting God all the way.

My husband walked in while I was on the phone with John. As I opened the conversation to him he was a bit quiet for a moment, in deep contemplation, I thought. He, as my pastor as well, was pleased that I was selected for such an office. He wholeheartedly supported me throughout my tenure as vice chair for the first year and then as chair in the second year.

During my year as vice chair (2013-2014) I was required to buddy the chairman, Rev Ian Todd of the Holy Saviour Church (Church of England). I am thankful for his mentorship. His calm demeanour helped me greatly to quickly settle in and to gradually develop the confidence to carry out my tasks. I was given my first 'public speaking' opportunity during this year as well. This was historic for me because since leaving Jamaica where I had only two opportunities to speak at graduations, this was a first for me in England; especially as the request came from people who hardly know me but yet saw something in me. This act made me instantly see the difference with my own church leaders. How fitting, as a migrant, I was asked to be guest speaker for the World Day of Prayer to address the theme 'I was a stranger and you welcomed me.'

My inauguration as chairman was on January 19th 2014. It was indeed an event which superseded my expectation. There was such great support from the people of our town. It was unbelievable, I was humbled by the experience. The St Mary's Parish Church was full to capacity. The encouragement and commendations I received that day was unprecedented. I was told that my sermon had a wide impact on the congregation that day. It was entitled 'Is Christ Divided?' And the recurring question which was accompanied by the audience's response 'No!' This still rings out on the lips of attendees even today. To God be the glory!

Given the challenges I had faced in my earlier Christian walk, in retrospect, It all makes sense now! The reality is that God had a plan for me and that the enemy of our souls was just not happy. Yes, it was very challenging for me but by God's grace I was able to get through this rough period of my life. Ironically, the night before my inauguration and a couple of weeks before my handing over one year later, I was faced with similar challenges from the same group of people – character assassination.

Thanks be to God for His divine protection and the power of forgiveness. The town's newspapers did not get the news the enemy had intended to be printed of me. Instead, the opposite happened. Thank the Lord! It all makes sense now!

Shortly following my inauguration I was invited to meet with Rev. Dr. Joe Aldred, director of Pentecostal and Multicultural Relations at Churches Together in England. I was accompanied by John, secretary to Churches Together in Hitchin and his lovely wife, Helen, to the CTE office in London. What an inspirational man of God he turned out to be! I was humbled and honoured to meet him. He encouraged me in my walk of faith and he enlightened me about church culture here in the UK which I found very useful in the end, as I could already relate. We also found out we belonged to the same denomination.

During our meeting Rev Joe also made reference to my inauguration sermon which he found 'inspiring and truthful with a good balance of scripture references'. His next statement was a real encouragement to me when he said that he even used 'a quotation from my sermon' in a lecture he gave to a group of university students that day. He quickly informed me that he did give credence to me. It really would not have mattered to me anyway. I am blessed to have met him!

The year as chairman was very fulfilling for me. I have been told by many people how my efforts have impacted them in one way or other; and by extension, impacted our town. Such compliments propelled me to give all the glory to God. It is His doing and it is marvellous in His eyes.

Among the activities I was involved in during the course of the year was hosting the Good Friday Walk of Witness in the town which was reported to be one of the best attendances ever seen. We were also blessed with fine weather. During that service I gave a Sign Language presentation to the Sandi Patty's song 'We

Shall Behold Him'. It appeared to have grabbed the attention of everyone around, even the shoppers who were passing by. I was told the use of Signed Language was quite unique. The commendations which followed were very humbling and encouraging for me.

Then there were other CTH events which I participated in. These included the Songs of Praise, which is a gathering of the churches in Hitchin to sing to the Lord. This was our first time participating in it and all were blessed by contribution. It was a blessing to see the performances of various churches. An evening of communal praise!

The co-ordinator of Song of Praise also coordinated the Party in the square, which saw all the churches coming together in the town square to share with the community. Each church had a stall and issued food and cakes for free along with bounce about and other fun items for the children. Our church also had a stall there. I was one of three people who were asked to share our testimony on that day.

Remembrance Service (WW1) was another moving historic event during that year. I participated as part of the planning process as well. It focused on remembering what happened on that fateful day when many citizens of our town lost their lives during world war one, one hundred years ago. Given the painful experiences we abstained from calling it a celebration rather a remembrance service. Many members of the affected families were invited to take part in the service.

One of the main highlights of my year as chairman of CTH was the opportunity I had to chair the MEP debate hosted by Christchurch. This event saw the prospective members of the European Parliament for East of England presenting their cases. At the end I took the opportunity to pray for these noble men and women. Not being political here, but the MEP from Hitchin did emerge the winner at the subsequent election. This experience of meeting parliamentarians brought back memories for me of the years I worked as a sign language interpreter in the Jamaican House of Parliament and for government officials many, many moons ago.

At the AGM and hand over service in November 2014 and January 2015, respectively, I was truly encouraged to hear the kind tributes given to me by so many people. My local church family was especially proud of what God did through me. To God be all the glory, great things He has done!

Another interesting thing which happened made me realise that God was not through with me yet. At our 50th year celebration meeting of the CTH council in February 2015 a special mention was made of a section in the minutes from the very first council meeting held fifty years prior. It was highlighted that the then leader had mentioned: 'We need to include members of ethnic minority churches in the executive body'. Secretary, John Richardson was proud to report that it has finally happened, although it took fifty years to have the first 'black chairman'. In essence it happens to add to the jubilee celebration of Churches Together in Hitchin.

Additionally, at the end of the 50th anniversary meeting I was approached by Rev Dr Callan Slipper Ecumenical Facilitator of Churches Together in Hertfordshire. He works on a county-wide basis. Not only did he applaud me on the service he was told I gave to CTH during my time as chairman and the lovely inauguration sermon I gave, but that he wanted to speak with me about being a panellist at the Go For Growth Conference he would be facilitating later that year. I could hardly believe what I was hearing. I was convinced that this is the Lord's doing!

After a subsequent visit from the reverend I was briefed on the requirements and his vision for the growth of the county's churches. The conference was held on 3rd October 2015 and I was a part of a five-member panel who spoke on church growth in our respective organisations. I was also asked to pray the closing prayer. He emphasised I should do it the 'Pentecostal way'. I was humbled and honoured for the opportunity to represent my God at such a forum, among bishops and leaders of traditional churches.

The Go For Growth Conference was a real blessing. To God be all the praise, honour and glory. I stand in awe of my Father God and His mighty working power in my life. Below is a paragraph from the conference's aftermath email I received from the facilitator, Rev. Dr. Callan Slipper (Oct 5 at 3:29 PM).

"Dear Jane,

Thank you so much for being on our Panel. You did an excellent job and several people commented to me how much they valued your input. I'm also grateful to you (and to God!) for the beautiful moment of prayer you offered."

Retrospection

In retrospect, I am beginning to make sense of my personal trials. No wonder I had to go through the 'shut-up syndrome' mentioned earlier in this book; and other challenges (for example character assassination) in order to develop my Godly character. The amazing thing is that God is still working on me. He is certainly not through with me yet. Thank you Jesus! It all makes sense now!

On this journey there were many lessons learned. There is no doubt an individual's upbringing does impact his or her personality. During tough times one's personality or deep inner self comes to the fore. Therefore, although the trusting young woman I am sadly was often taken for granted, there is a supreme God who watches out for the vulnerable. Now I can keep believing the best in others. Determination and commitment are also end products. I glorify God for these qualities. It all makes sense now!

Cultures differ in ways that are unimaginable; even church culture. It is beneficial to come to grips with the differences as quickly as possible in order to lead a happier and more fulfilled life. Once there was an understanding of these differences it became easier to be accepted or to make sense of. It all makes sense now!

One thing that underpinned many of the testimonies shared is the 'power of forgiveness'. Forgiveness goes way beyond what a person feels. This is easily proven because very often one does not feel like forgiving the perpetrator. It is my belief that forgiveness comes by faith. In other words, it takes faith to forgive. Worthy of note too is the fact that forgiveness was required over and over again. This places the person forgiving in a position of faith, power and love.

It is in retrospection that many life lessons are deemed to be learned. Having gone through trials of one sort or another has allowed me time for reflection, reviewing the highs and lows. During these times emotions have calmed and a clearer perspective can be had on particular events. In retrospect, I give all the glory to God for guiding me through the good and the bad times.

My remarkable visitor on that stormy day must have been God sent. Praise God! It all makes sense now!

Photos

My Inaguration as chair of Churches Together in
Hitchin (Janurary 2014)

Someone gave this framed photo to me for my birthday
a week later.

Preaching the inauguration sermon 'Is Christ Divided?'

My Family shares in the moment

With CTH secretary Minister John Richardson

Chairing Member of European Parliament (MEP)
Debate for East of England
(Five parties present)

Both - Chairing MEP's Polical Debate (May 2014)

Moderating Good Friday Walk of Witness Service in
Hitchin town centre (April 2014)

Speaking at Hitchin Christian Fellowship as chair of
CTH (Sept 2014).

Master's Graduation (2009)

Sign Language Ministry (2008) – Speaking Hands,
Listening Eyes

Signing at Good Friday Walk of Witness Service in
Hitchin (2014)

Lightning Source UK Ltd.
Milton Keynes UK
UKOW02f0817010217
293343UK00002B/67/P